Thinking Deeper

Social Issues, Problems, and Solutions

Critical Thinking Discussion Activities

Second Edition

by John Spiri

Pro Lingua Associates

Pro Lingua Associates, Publishers
74 Cotton Mill Hill, Suite A 315
Brattleboro, Vermont 05301 USA
Office: 802-257-7779
Orders: 800-366-4775
Email: info@ProLinguaAssociates.com
WebStore: www.ProLinguaAssociates.com
SAN: 216-0579

At Pro Lingua
our objective is to foster an approach
to learning and teaching that we call
***interplay**, the **inter**action of language*
learners and teachers with their materials,
with the language and culture,
and with each other in active, creative,
*and productive **play**.*

ISBN 978-0-86647-494-8

Thinking Deeper was designed by John Spiri. It was set in Palatino, the most widely used, and pirated, face of the twentieth century, which was designed by Hermann Zapf in 1948 in Frankfurt. Although modern, it is based on Renaissance designs typical of the Palatinate area in Germany.

Photo Credits: Front cover © Mark Adams/Dreamstime; back cover @ Vadymvdro/Dreamstime; red leather © Banprick/Dreamstime; title page © Mark Adams/Dreamstime; ii © Denys Kovtun/ Dreamstime; 8 © People for Care and Learning; 14 © londondeposit (Craig Robinson); 18 © aijohn784 (John Roman); 22 human rights - © Kashmir Global; 23 © lightsource; 24 Junk food © kentannenbaum/Dreamstime; 25 © Diego Cervo; 28 © prometeus (Kiselev Andrey); 30 © konstantynov; 31 © TarasMalyarevich; 33 © yanlev (Alexey Sizov); 34 © ilfede; 35 Muslim woman © zurijeta; 37 Eiffel Tower © Tristan Nitot; 38 © Danny Choo; 39 © Pavel Svoboda Photography; 40 dad and daughter © Kim Davies, mother with son © Yu; 41 adulthood © Martin Novak/Dreamstime; 42 chores © Old Horseradish; 45 ethics © Drew McKissick; 46 David © Gkasabova; 47 Larry © Angelo Cordeschi, Phil © Ridel; 59 © NASA.
All other images are either the author's, stock photos, or from Wiki Commons. The publisher has endeavored to trace all the copyright holders of images included in this book. If we have inadvertently omitted anything, please contact us and we will make the necessary arrangements.

The book was printed and bound by Royal Palm Press in Punta Gorda, Florida.

Printed in the United States of America

Second Edition, first printing 2019

Contents

Thinking Deeper: Social Issues, Problems, and Solutions

Introduction

Critical Thinking Discussion Activites

This collection of 61 copyable thinking/discussion activities features a wide variety of critically important contemporary social issues, problems, and solutions that affect every citizen of Planet Earth. It is aimed at a young adult and adult audience of English language learners at an intermediate and higher proficiency level. With some adaptation it can also be used selectively with middle school students.

For English language learners, there are two main purposes to these activities. First: Practicing English language skills, especially the skills of speaking and listening, in a conversation where learners also develop strategic competency as they engage in the back and forth of a discussion. Second: As the title suggests, learners are asked to think about the positions they will take as they do the activity. In today's world, more than ever, it is imperative that citizenry think beyond platitudes, slogans, and political promises, and have the opportunity to develop and explore their views on issues of local and global importance.

Although originally designed for English language learners, the simple design of the page and the procedures of the activities make this photocopyable resource appropriate for a variety of classrooms, including those where English is the first language and the main focus is the critical thinking objective.

User's Guide

Decide when to use this resource. These activities can supplement many themes of a class plan or curriculum. In addition, this resource can be used independently, with the teacher or the learners choosing an activity each week. Depending on learners' abilities to comprehend it and express themselves, and the time available in a class, an activity may take anywhere from 15 minutes to an hour or more.

Explain why. First and foremost, the users need to understand, putting it simply, why they are doing the activities. As part of your introduction, it may be helpful to give them a copy of the table of contents to increase their interest and motivation to engage in this wide variety of topics. It may also be helpful to have them prioritize the sequence of the activities.

Explain Critical Thinking. Explain that, as we explore these contemporary issues, we are also working on our critical thinking skills. Introduce the Quick Checklist on page viii, which may be used after each unit. Note that a fuller explanation of the five strategies is available on vii, and that there is a complete list of 35 strategies on page 62.

Build schema. After selecting and copying an activity page, and even before handing it out, conduct a brief "What do you know about ..." to get things started. Of course, this can also be done as the page is handed out. Be sure to read through the discussion points to notice information that may need explanation.

Read the topic statement. Although you can have learners read the opening statement silently, there is some advantage to reading it aloud as they follow along or read aloud with you in a quiet voice. Encourage them to consider the pictures. This will start them thinking about the issue. Then everyone is "on the same page" when you have finished reading, and they can be launched into using the scale to establish their points of view.

Read the discussion points (optional). The learners are asked to rate the discussion points according to the scale. Depending on the proficiency level of the participants, it might be useful to read the discussion points aloud, soliciting questions about the vocabulary. You can also have the learners take turns reading the discussion points aloud. Then everyone is ready to begin their prioritizing at the same time.

Rating the discussion points. It could be advisable to establish a time limit to this step so that all are ready to begin the discussion at about the same time.

Share and discuss. Working in small groups gives participants sufficient opportunity to express their ideas. Groups of four usually work well. Learners may also work in pairs. Set a time limit for the discussion. Give the participants a "two-minute warning" before wrapping up the activity. A final step can be to have each group share some of what they discussed with the other groups.

Another way to wrap up is to take a class survey. You can collapse a ten-point scale by writing on the board "0-3" (low support or whatever), "4-6" (medium), and "7-10" (strong support or whatever). After listing the activity items you'd like to focus on, have learners raise hands to show their level of support for each, and tally for each of the 3 scale groupings.

When the discussions are finished, you can further explore the groups' decisions by using the Survey form on page 64. Have the learners select 5 points and then poll the group to see how they rated the discussion points.

Finally, after the discussions, have the learner use the Critical Thinking Quick Checklist, reflecting on their own thinking.

Research and/or write (optional). You can have learners write a brief summary of their positions on one or more of the points raised in the activities. Alternatively, you can provide internet address suggestions for a follow-up. The participants check the internet for homework, report the next day on what they found, or write a brief summary of what they found and how it did or didn't affect their views.

Critical Thinking: Five Strategies

A quick checklist, found on page viii, summarizes the 5 strategies below. For the full checklist of 35 strategies, see page 62. They are adapted from the 35 strategies listed under ***"Dimensions of Critical Thought"*** *by* **The Foundation for Critical Thinking**.

1. Think independently: Critical thinkers use skills and insights to reject beliefs that are irrational. In forming new beliefs, critical thinkers do not passively accept the beliefs of others; rather, they figure things out for themselves, reject unjustified authorities, and recognize true authorities. They are not easily manipulated. Critical thinkers determine for themselves when information is relevant, when to apply a concept, or when to make use of a skill. They are self-monitoring: they catch their own mistakes.

2. Fairness: Fairness requires remembering times when we were wrong in the past despite a strong belief that we were right. The world consists of many societies and peoples with many different points of view and ways of thinking. To develop as reasonable persons, we need to consider and appreciate the ideas of different peoples and societies. We cannot truly understand the world if we think about it only from one viewpoint, as Americans, as Japanese, or as Brazilians. Furthermore, critical thinkers consider their behavior from the perspective of others.

3. Reasons: We can better understand our feelings by asking ourselves, "Why do I feel this way? How am I looking at the situation? What is my evidence? What assumptions am I making? Are there other ways to interpret this situation?" Understanding ourselves is the first step toward self-control and self-improvement. This self-understanding requires that we understand our feelings and emotions in relation to our thoughts, ideas, and interpretations of the world.

4. Credibility: Critical thinkers recognize the importance of using reliable sources of information. They are careful about using sources which have, in the past, lacked honesty. They avoid sources that have a separate motive (like making money). Critical thinkers recognize when there is more than one reasonable position on an issue; they compare different sources of information, noting areas of agreement; and they gather more information when sources disagree. They realize that our ideas influence observations–we often see only what we expect to see and fail to notice things we aren't looking for.

5. Analyze and evaluate: Rather than quickly agreeing or disagreeing with a conclusion based on opinions of what is true, critical thinkers use analysis to understand the reasoning behind a conclusion and determine its strengths and weaknesses. Critical thinkers are especially sensitive to arguments that they disagree with, recognizing the tendency to ignore, oversimplify, distort, or otherwise unfairly reject them. Critical thinkers explore the assumptions on which interpretations are based and propose and evaluate alternative interpretations.

Five Critical Thinking Strategies
Quick Checklist

Did you...

1. think independently? **yes no**
2. make and express your view with an attitude of fairness? **yes no**
3. explore your reasons for thinking and feeling the way you did? **yes no**
4. evaluate the credibility of sources of information? **yes no**
5. analyze and evaluate arguments, interpretations, beliefs, or theories? **yes no**

1. Thinking Deeper about

Homelessness

Why do people become homeless? Do people become homeless because of economic conditions? Poor government? Poor personal choices? Think about these pictures.

Write a number to rank each potential cause of homelessness below.

The Scale

Ten-point scale question: To what extent are the problems below a cause of homelessness?

0	1	2	3	4	5	6	7	8	9	10
(not at all)		*(slightly)*			*(somewhat)*		*(very much)*			*(most)*

Potential Cause	Brief Description and/or Examples
1. alcoholism __	regularly overdrinking so it negatively affects life
2. drug addiction __	can't stop taking cocaine, heroin, etc.
3. unemployment __	out of work
4. mental illness __	severe depression, anxiety disorders, etc.
5. physical disability __	a serious injury or disease
6. overpopulation __	too many people in a city, in a country, or on Earth
7. desire to live outside __	a person refuses to stay in a shelter
8. laziness __	no energy or motivation to work
9. low wages __	hourly pay is too low
10. bankruptcy __	a business has to close forever
11. grief __	great sadness due to the loss of a loved one
12. despair __	losing all hope to live
13. isolation __	no family or community support
14. taxation __	taxes are too high

When finished, share your ratings with your partners. Finally, use the checklist on page viii.

2. Thinking Deeper about
Bullying

"Bullying" often means a physical attack or threat. However, people sometimes bully with words only. How should people in authority—teachers, parents, and other adults—deal with bullying? Should they punish the bully? Should they focus on helping the victim? Should they stay out of the situation? Can other youth make a difference? Rate each potential solution for bullying below.

The Scale

Ten-point scale question: To what extent do you recommend the bullying solutions below?

0	1	2	3	4	5	6	7	8	9	10
(completely ineffective)...		*(a little)...*			*(somewhat)...*		*(very effective)*			*(most)*

1. All students discuss a bullying incident together with the teacher __
2. The victim fights back against the bully, punching or kicking him __
3. Others ignore the situation, believing the bully and victim will work it out themselves __
4. An adult makes the bully apologize to the victim __
5. An adult calls the bully's parents to discuss the situation __
6. A classmate tells the bully to stop __
7. Teach the victim karate or other form of self-defense __
8. Punish the bully by making them research and write about bullying __
9. Suspend the bully from school for one week __
10. Get counseling for the victim __
11. Call the police if the bullying is physical or involves threats __
12. Teach bullies to feel empathy __

When finished, share your ratings and reasons and discuss them with your partners.

3. Thinking Deeper about
Gender Roles

Our social environment plays a big role in how we develop and act as adults. People have strong ideas about what it means to be a man, and what it means to be a woman. These beliefs may be conscious or unconscious. Consider your views on gender by completing the scale below.

The Scale: *What do you think about the questions below? Rate on a scale of 0 to 10.*

0	1	2	3	4	5	6	7	8	9	10
(no way!)		*(probably not)*			*(maybe yes maybe no)*			*(probably)*		*(definitely!)*

1. Would it be better if women wore makeup less or not at all? __
2. Would it be a positive development if most men started regularly wearing makeup? __
3. Is it wise for a woman to have cosmetic surgery to maintain a youthful appearance? __
4. Is it wise for men to lift weights and take supplements to get huge muscles? __
5. Do you prefer to see women wearing women's clothing (skirts, dresses, etc.)? __
6. Should it be socially acceptable for men to wear women's clothing (skirts, etc.)? __
7. Are women who paint their fingernails more attractive? __
8. Can a woman's hairy legs be as attractive as her clean-shaven legs? __
9. Should schools allow boys to have long hair? __
10. Are women better than men at taking care of infants? __
11. Do men, in general, have greater creative energy to make music, art, etc.? __
12. Are women stronger than men at enduring pain and discomfort? __
13. Should boys be taught to be tough and not cry? __
14. Is it strange for women to hunt and kill wild animals? __
15. Should adults strongly discourage or punish 10-year-old boys who have fist fights? __
16. Should 16-year-old girls be allowed to play contact sports like boxing? __
17. Would you feel comfortable in a marriage that mainly relies on the wife's income? __
18. Would you feel comfortable in a marriage where the man is a "househusband"? __
19. Should women be accepted as soldiers and fight in wars? __
20. Are there only two genders, male and female, or could there be more genders? __

When finished, discuss your answers with your partners.

4. Thinking Deeper about

Discrimination

People might be treated unfairly, and discriminated against, for many reasons. In your society, to what extent do minorities get discriminated against? What about women? The elderly? Think about the picture below, and then rate each potential reason for discrimination.

The Scale

How troubling is each situation below? Rate them.

0	1	2	3	4	5	6	7	8	9	10
(not discrimination)			*(a little)*		*(somewhat)*		*(very troubling)*			*(worst)*

1. Sex: few women get construction jobs, supposedly due to a lack of strength __
2. Sex: an interviewer asks a woman if she plans to have children __
3. Sex: a politician says infants need their mother more than their father __
4. Sex: young men are forced to fight in wars while women are not __
5. Age: a productive worker is forced to retire at 65 __
6. Race: a hot spring spa doesn't allow foreigners because they might not wash first __
7. Race: a foreigner cannot rent an apartment because he is not Japanese __
8. Nationality: an immigrant is paid less money than a local doing the same factory job __
9. Profiling: police in Arizona stop people who look Hispanic and check them for drugs __
10. Profiling: it is harder for Muslims to get refugee status than people of other religions __
11. Religion: Muslims are screened more carefully at airport immigration and customs __
12. Religion: all religious symbols like Islamic veils and head-scarves are banned __
13. Poverty: more poor people go to prison than rich even though the crime rate is the same __
14. Occupational: people avoid speaking with low-status workers like janitors __
15. Appearance: a better qualified but less attractive person doesn't get a job __
16. Mental challenges: a person with Down Syndrome can't get a cashier's job __
17. Physical challenges: a person in a wheelchair cannot enter a building with no ramp __
18. Sexuality: a gay man can't marry his lover __
19. Identity: a man who identifies as a woman is not allowed to use the women's toilet __

When finished, share your ratings and reasons and discuss them with your partners.

5. Thinking Deeper about

Equality

Are men and women treated equally in your society? Are there any situations where unequal treatment is desirable? Think about the picture, and then rate the situations below.

The Scale

How fairly or unfairly are women or men treated in the situations below? Rate from -10 to 0 to 10.

-10 — -8 — -6 — -4 — -2 — 0 — 2 — 4 — 6 — 8 — 10

(most unfair to men) *(not a question of fairness)* *(most unfair to women)*

the situation	rank	reason for your opinion
1. Imagine a couple where the husband and wife have similar jobs working similar hours. They divide housework and childcare evenly.		
2. A male and female employee each have equal ability and work equal hours. The man is promoted to a higher position in the company.		
3. Male customers pay **more** while females pay **less** for an "all-you-can-eat" buffet at a Japanese restaurant.		
4. In some countries, women must cover their faces, or their entire heads, with a hijab (a cloth) in public.		
5. In some countries, men must have a beard.		
6. At certain hours, men are not allowed to ride on "Women Only" train cars in Japan.		
7. In some countries women are not allowed to stay in school past 3rd grade. Instead, they learn to cook and do housework.		
8. Only women can get pregnant.		

When finished, discuss your ratings and ideas with your partners.

6. Thinking Deeper about
Harassment

People's awareness of sexual harassment, and recognizing it as a problem in the workplace, began in the 1970s. Since then, other kinds of harassment have been identified. What actions can be called "harassment"? Rate the situations described below.

The Scale

How troubling is each situation of harassment below? Rate on a scale of 0 to 10.

0	1	2	3	4	5	6	7	8	9	10
(no problem)		*(a little troubling)*			*(medium)*		*(troubling)*		*(most troubling)*	

1. A boss keeps greeting his secretary "Hi, honey" even after she asked him to stop. __
2. A man keeps calling a Mexican colleague "Mexico" instead of his actual name. __
3. A boss tells a receptionist the company needs "a beautiful woman like you" at the front.
4. A male teacher taps a female student on the shoulder to get her attention in class. __
5. Keiko massages a male colleague in a shared office. The male colleague likes it. __
6. Jim, unmarried at 55, laughs when asked by Asako, "Have you ever had sex?" __
7. A boss keeps asking a worker out on a date, hinting that it could lead to a promotion. __
8. A female construction worker gets jokingly asked, "What color are your panties?" __
9. A male politician pats a female friend's behind as they stand for a photograph. __
10. A boss who has a side business selling New Year's food specialties tells his workers they must buy two for $200 each. __
11. Bill gets yelled at by his boss for talking about sports during lunchtime. __
12. When Ann walks down the street in a mini-skirt and tight blouse, men whistle at her. __
13. When Jack calls his coworker Janet "beautiful" she smiles warmly. __
14. Brad gets a pay cut at his international university because he suggested the university president replace the national flag with an Earth flag. __
15. A senior university student forces a junior to chug a whiskey and a beer. __

Share your ratings and discuss your opinions with your partners.

7. Thinking Deeper about
Environmental Problems

After Rachel Carson wrote Silent Spring *in 1962, people became more aware of environmental problems. Today, the list of problems has grown long. Which environmental problems are most troubling? Rate the problems below.*

The Scale: *How troubling is each environmental problem below? Rate on a scale of 0 to 10.*

0	1	2	3	4	5	6	7	8	9	10
(no problem)		*(a little troubling)*			*(somewhat)*		*(troubling)*		*(most troubling)*	

1. Rainforest trees are cut down to make farms. __
2. Large mammals like tigers are endangered. __
3. Bees are disappearing. __
4. Air pollution in big cities has become harmful to health. __
5. Lake and river water is too polluted to drink or swim in. __
6. Farmers and citizens use so much underground water that the ground is sinking. __
7. Traffic is noisy so people can't sleep at night. __
8. Billboards (advertisement boards) are so large we can't see scenery. __
9. Nuclear power plants must pay other countries to store dangerous waste. __
10. Soil blows away, decreasing agricultural land while desert areas are expanding. __
11. The average temperature is getting higher every year due to climate change. __
12. When certain man-made gasses reach the upper parts of the atmosphere, they cause a hole in the ozone layer, especially over the Antarctic. __
13. World population will increase from 7 billion to 10 billion by 2060. __
14. People litter by throwing platic bags, empty bottles, and other trash onto streets. __
15. The Great Pacific Garbage Patch in the Pacific Ocean mainly contains plastic waste. __
16. Forests are cut down to build shopping malls. __
17. Space debris may harm spacecrafts and satellites or crash onto Earth. __

Make sure you understand each issue by discussing it with your partners. Is there a danger to humans? Is there a danger to other animals? Also discuss the ones you find most troubling. Explain why.

8. Thinking Deeper about
Waste Disposal

Citizens of developed countries create a lot of trash and other waste. How does it get disposed of? Where does it go?

The Scale

What are the best ways to deal with waste? Rate the ideas below from 0 to 10.

0	1	2	3	4	5	6	7	8	9	10
(worst)		*(not so good)*			*(so-so)*		*(pretty good)*			*(best)*

1. Bury trash under the ground in landfills. __
2. Incinerate trash by burning it at high temperatures. __
3. Break trash down (for example, melt plastic) and recycle it into new products. __
4. Compost food scraps and use them as fertilizer in a garden. __
5. Raise pigs for the purpose of eating garbage. __
6. Throw your trash out your car window when nobody is looking. __
7. Give poorer countries cash to accept shipments of nuclear waste. __
8. Make an entire amusement park from trash, as Ruganzu Bruno did in Uganda. __
9. Bury nuclear waste deep underground in or near your hometown. __
10. Always bring your own bags to stores. __
11. Only buy what you need. __
12. Get your shoes and other goods repaired instead of buying new ones. __
13. Always recycle. __
14. Live off the land by eating wild plants and berries and not buying anything. __

Share your ratings and discuss your opinions with your partners.

9. Thinking Deeper about

Environmental Solutions

Humans are very successful. However, as we consume more and more, and use more space, the natural environment is harmed. What are the most promising environmental solutions?

The Scale

How promising are the environmental solutions below? Rate them using the scale.

0 — 1 — 2 — 3 — 4 — 5 — 6 — 7 — 8 — 9 — 10

(worst solution) (at 0) … *(medium)* (at 5) … *(best solution)* (at 10)

environmental issue	**potential solution**
1. animal extinction	a) shoot to kill poachers (those who hunt illegally) __
2. dead sea zones	b) greatly reduce chemical fertilizer use in agriculture __
3. Great Pacific Garbage Patch	c) invent a machine to suck it up __
4. overfishing	d) set strict limits on what fishermen can catch __
5. excess garbage	e) recycle extensively __
6. pesticide poisoning	f) promote organic foods __
7. desertification	g) plant trees to keep soil from blowing away __
8. overpopulation	h) prohibit having more than one child __
9. pollution	i) give penalties for making air or water dirty __
10. climate change	j) develop green energy (solar, wind, etc.) __
11. destruction of coral reefs	k) prohibit people from going in seas near coral __
12. deforestation	l) plant trees __
13. space debris	m) build Necropolis to collect space trash and store it __

Compare your numbers for both the problem and solution, and discuss them with partners.

10. Thinking Deeper about
Protests

Protesters hope to bring attention to an issue. Then, more importantly, they hope to make positive changes to society.

Gandhi encouraged Indians to make their own clothing using a spinning wheel, pictured above, and a loom.

The Scale

To what extent do you support the protests below? Rate on a scale of 0 to 10.

0	1	2	3	4	5	6	7	8	9	10
(no support)		*(a little)*			*(some)*		*(strong)*			*(strongest)*

1. John Lennon and Yoko Ono staged a "Bed-in," staying in bed for two weeks for peace. __
2. An Iraqi journalist threw a shoe at President Bush because the U.S. started the Iraq War. __
3. Indian women started the Chipko Movement by hugging trees to protect them. __
4. In the early 1900s, Indians boycotted clothes made by British companies. __
5. Environmentalists harassed Japanese ships that were hunting whales. __
6. When a police officer asked a foreigner, who was innocently walking the street, to show his alien registration card, the foreigner refused. __
7. In 2017, millions of people walked with signs to protest the election of Donald Trump and support women's rights, environmental protection, healthcare reform, etc. __
8. After citizens discovered the U.S. had lied and was bombing Cambodia during the Vietnam War, students at Kent State University in Ohio protested. __
9. In 2008, "yellow-shirt" protesters took control of Bangkok airport to force the Thai president to quit. No planes could fly, so travelers were stuck for many days. __
10. In 1773, protesters in Boston destroyed an entire shipment of tea to protest the Tea Act that required American colonists to pay what they considered to be an illegal British tax on tea. __
11. 125,000 French protesters, angry about rising living costs, clashed with 90,000 police. __
12. NFL football players refused to stand up for the U.S. national anthem to protest social injustice. __

Discuss your ratings with a partner.

11. Thinking Deeper about
Civil Disobedience

Breaking the law is usually considered wrong. But what about when the law is not just? When is breaking the law acceptable, if ever? Rank the situations below.

the "Tank Man" at Tiananmen Square

Rosa Parks

The Scale: *To what extent do you support the examples of civil disobedience below?*

0 — 1 — 2 — 3 — 4 — 5 — 6 — 7 — 8 — 9 — 10

(no support) (0) · *(a little)* (2–3) · *(some)* (5) · *(strong)* (7–8) · *(strongest)* (10)

1. Julia Butterfly Hill lived in a tree, to save it. Environmentalists supported her. She came down two years later after the timber company agreed to save the tree. ___
2. In 1955 in Alabama in the U.S. south, Rosa Parks, who was sitting in the "colored" section of a city bus, refused to give up her seat to a white man. She was arrested. ___
3. In 1893, Gandhi was told to give up his train seat because of his race. He refused. ___
4. Under British rule, Indians were prohibited from collecting or selling salt. In 1930, Gandhi and his supporters walked hundreds of kilometers to the sea. Over 60,000 Indians were arrested for collecting sea salt. Some were beaten. ___
5. Ben Griffin, a British soldier, refused to continue fighting the Iraq War in 2005 because he felt the war was unjust. ___
6. To protect Jews trying to escape Nazis in the early 1940s, Chiune Sugihara wrote fake visas to help them find a safe country. ___
7. Environmentalists secretly videoed fishermen clubbing many dolphins to death in Wakayama in 2014. The sea was red with dolphin blood. The videos were shared online. ___
8. To protect Jews from Nazis, Oskar Schindler hid them in his factory. ___
9. The "Tank Man," an unidentified Chinese protester, stood in front of a tank to block it from advancing during the Tiananmen Square protests in 1989.
10. 150 Tibetans have burned themselves to death because China is occupying Tibet. ___

When finished, discuss with a partner. Why did people do these acts of civil disobedience? What do they want? Would some other protest action have been more effective? Think of the point of view of both the protester and the other side.

12. Thinking Deeper about
Punishments

How can bad behavior be stopped? Parents, teachers, and governments, all decide punishments. When is a punishment wise? When is it unwise?

How appropriate are the punishments below? Rate from -10 to 0 to 10.

-10 -8 -6 -4 -2 0 2 4 6 8 10

(most inappropriate) *(not bad or good)* *(most appropriate)*

1. A parent spanks a child's behind (aged 1-3) ___ (aged 4-7) ___
2. A parent slaps a child's face (aged 1-3) ___ (aged 4-7) ___
3. A parent slaps a child's hand (aged 1-3) ___ (aged 4-7) ___
4. A parent temporarily takes away a favorite toy ___
5. A parent denies a 6-year-old dinner ___
6. A parent locks a 7-year-old outside (in a safe yard) for one hour ___
7. Parents drive away from their 6-year-old on a country road for five minutes ___
8. A teacher kicks a student out of class for constantly bothering classmates ___
9. A principal expels a high school student for 2 weeks for smoking in school ___
10. Police question a suspect 16 hours a day for two weeks to get a confession ___
11. Police beat a man suspected of murder to get a confession ___
12. Soldiers torture an enemy soldier to get information about a terror attack ___
13. A judge sentences a mass murderer to life in prison ___
14. The state executes a man who was found guilty of murder ___
15. A speeder is fined $800 for driving 15 miles per hour over the speed limit ___
16. An angry mob cuts off a thief's arm ___
17. A murderer is forced to live in an apartment on an island prison where he lives pretty much a normal life and travels to the city to work on weekends ___

Share your answers with your partners, telling why you think the punishment is or isn't appropriate.

13. Thinking Deeper about
Crime

Societies need ways to deal with crime. There's an English saying, "The punishment should fit the crime." What punishments are appropriate for the crimes below?

The Scale

Rank how severe the punishment should be for the crimes below.

0	1	2	3	4	5	6	7	8	9	10
(least severe)		*(a little severe)*			*(reasonable)*		*(severe)*		*(most severe)*	

Crime	Example of crime
1. poaching	Poachers hunt and kill endangered mountain gorillas in Africa __
2. drug trafficking	Criminals smuggle cocaine into Thailand __
3. human trafficking	The mafia brings girls into a country to be prostitutes __
4. terrorism	Terrorists plan and execute airplane hijackings on 9/11 __
5. rape	A man forces sex on a woman __
6. perversion	A pervert grabs a woman's behind on a train __
7. attempted murder	A man tries, but fails, to kill someone __
8. random murder	A man kills five students and a teacher at a high school __
9. robbery	Robbers use a gun to demand money in a bank __
10. drunk driving	A young man drives a car after drinking six beers __
11. kidnapping	A man forcibly takes a child and demands money __
12. fraud	A man scams elderly of millions of dollars by pretending to be a grandchild and saying "It's me, It's me. I need money." __
13. drug abuse	An addict injects heroin every day __
14. trespassing	A hiker walks across privately owned land __
15. theft	A man cuts down a tree in a privately owned forest __
16. copyright violation	A young woman downloads a song without paying for it __

Share your ratings and discuss them with your partners.

14. Thinking Deeper about
Weapons

Most weapons are designed to kill. Still, some people think weapons should be freely available so citizens can defend themselves from criminals, terrorists, and even the government. Others think weapons should be strictly controlled.

Cluster bombs are small bombs dropped out of a shell.

The Scale

Rate how dangerous each weapon is and its usefulness. Then write whether it should be banned.

-10 -8 -6 -4 -2 0 2 4 6 8 10

(most dangerous/useless) *(somewhat)* *(safest/most useful)*

	danger rank	usefulness rank	ban it? (write "yes" or "no")
1. bow and arrow	____	____	____
2. handgun	____	____	____
3. nuclear bomb	____	____	____
4. landmine	____	____	____
5. pepper spray	____	____	____
6. kitchen knife	____	____	____
7. pocket knife	____	____	____
8. rifle / shotgun for hunting	____	____	____
9. cluster bombs (see above right)	____	____	____
10. semi-automatic weapon*	____	____	____
11. automatic weapons**	____	____	____

** Fires each time the trigger is pressed, and automatically prepares to fire again.*

*** Can continually shoot as long as the trigger is pressed, between 3 and 1,800 bullets a minute.*

When finished, share your ratings and discuss with a partner.

15. Thinking Deeper about
Conflicts

Countries, like individuals, experience conflicts. What are the causes and solutions for conflicts? If time allows, read online about some of the conflicts below. Try "Simple Wikipedia."

The Scale

To what extent do you agree with the proposals below?

-10	-8	-6	-4	-2	0	2	4	6	8	10
(completely disagree)					*(neutral)*					*(completely agree)*

1. China, which took control of Tibet in 1949, should leave and let Tibet be independent. __
2. Israel needs to control the Gaza Strip for its safety. __
3. Gaza should be its own country because the Israeli occupation is causing suffering. __
4. More countries should move their embassy in Israel from Tel Aviv to Jerusalem. __
5. Catalonia, a wealthy and productive region with a unique history, wants independence from Spain. Barcelona is located in Catalonia. __
6. The U.S. should punish Russia for their apparent meddling in the 2016 election. __
7. Countries should bomb and destroy North Korea's nuclear weapons facilities. __
8. The U.S. and Korea should not conduct military exercises near North Korea. __
9. The U.S. should close its military bases in Okinawa. __
10. When Somali pirates take a ship's crew hostage, the company that owns the ship should never pay money to free them. __
11. Japan should stop hunting whales in the Southern Ocean. __
12. The Canadian and U.S. governments should not build or use the Keystone Pipeline. __
13. Russia needs soldiers in Ukraine to defend Crimea, which they took in 2014. __
14. Quebec should vote to separate from Canada and be an independent country. __

When finished, share your ratings and discuss with a partner.

16. Thinking Deeper about
Wars

Some people, like historians, spend their lives studying the causes of particular wars. Citizens learn about their country's wars in school but the lessons might not always be complete or accurate. What are your impressions and opinions about the war situations described below?

The Scale

What do you think about the way the wars below are described? Rate on a scale of 0 to 10.

0	1	2	3	4	5	6	7	8	9	10
(no way!)		*(probably not)*		*(maybe yes maybe no)*			*(probably)*		*(definitely!)*	

1. When Kublai Khan invaded Japan in 1274, a kamikaze wind sank their ships, saving Japan. The *kami*, the gods of Japan, caused the wind. __
2. The colonists were justified in fighting Great Britain in 1775 to gain independence. __
3. In the Vietnam War, North Vietnam was attempting to make the world communist. __
4. Ho Chi Minh was trying to liberate Vietnam from American influence. __
5. The U.S. should continue killing suspected terrorists in Pakistan with drones. __
6. 911 was "blowback," a natural reaction by Islamic individuals, because the U.S. was a bad influence in the Middle East and wanted to control their resources, like oil. __
7. Islamic terrorists attacked the U.S. on 9/11 because they hate America for its freedom. __
8. Japan was responsible for starting the Pacific Theater of World War II. The allies were innocent. __
9. Dropping atomic bombs on Hiroshima and Nagasaki was a U.S. war crime. __
10. Koreans were innocent victims of Japanese aggression before and during World War II. __
11. The separation of Korea into North and South after World War II is a great historical injustice. __
12. Only the presence of the U.S. military is stopping North Korea from attacking the South. __
13. The trials of Hideki Tojo and other "war criminals" after World War II were unfair. __
14. There will be World War III by the year 2100. __

When finished, share your ratings and discuss with a partner.

17. Thinking Deeper about

The Causes of War

Humans have been fighting wars for a very long time. Some animals, like chimpanzees, fight small-scale wars. Is the cause of war human nature? Injustice? Ignorance?

Write a number to rate each possible cause of war below.

The Scale

To what extent is each point below a cause of war?

0	1	2	3	4	5	6	7	8	9	10
(not at all)		*(slightly)*			*(somewhat)*		*(very much)*			*(most)*

Potential Cause	**Brief Description and/or Examples**
1. greed __	citizens want too many material goods and comforts
2. fear __	citizens are afraid of other countries
3. religion __	groups think their god is greatest or the only true god
4. nationalism __	citizens love their own country more than others
5. propaganda __	misinformation; lies spread by the government or media
6. poverty __	a lack of food and money
7. ignorance __	citizens lack intelligence and knowledge
8. imperialism __	a powerful country takes control of another region or country
9. resources __	a country wants more precious resources like water or minerals
10. militarism __	too many guns, bombs, etc. that a country is eager to use
11. governments __	politicians want more power, territory, etc.
12. soldiers __	soldiers always obey commands to kill "enemies"
13. history __	past problems were never solved and past events lead to war
14. bias __	people mainly interpret events from their own point of view

When finished, share your ratings and discuss with a partner.

18. Thinking Deeper about
Dangerous Jobs

Some people risk their lives at work. Which jobs do you think are most dangerous? What makes them dangerous? Rate the jobs below.

The Scale

How dangerous is each of the jobs below? Rate them; then write the job's greatest danger.

0	1	2	3	4	5	6	7	8	9	10
(no danger)					*(some danger)*					*(most dangerous)*

job	rate	job's greatest danger
1. reporter		
2. carpenter		
3. dentist		
4. construction worker		
5. farmer		
6. firefighter		
7. police officer		
8. librarian		
9. astronaut		
10. coal miner		
11. cashier		
12. university professor		
13. Sherpa mountain guide		
14. taxi driver		
15. deep-sea fisherman		

Share and discuss your answers with your partners.

19. Thinking Deeper about
Poverty

Some people, and communities, do not have enough food and material goods to survive. Others are barely surviving while a few are very wealthy.

The Scale

To what extent is each point below a cause of poverty?

0	1	2	3	4	5	6	7	8	9	10
(not at all)		*(slightly)*			*(somewhat)*		*(very much)*		*(greatest)*	

Potential Cause	**Brief Description and/or Examples**
1. discrimination __	mistreatment because of race, sex, etc.
2. age __	people are too old or too young
3. family size __	a couple has too many children
4. physical disability __	a problem with the body
5. laziness __	not working even though a person is capable
6. economic depression __	not enough jobs or money in society
7. lack of education __	a person didn't graduate or learn enough
8. corruption __	government leaders are taking too much or stealing
9. history __	former colonies had many of their resources taken
10. debt __	poor countries owe a lot of money and interest on loans
11. civil war __	groups within a country are fighting
12. low wages __	hourly pay is not enough
13. climate __	not enough rain or too many natural disasters

When finished, share your ratings and discuss with a partner.

20. Thinking Deeper about
Natural Disasters

A natural disaster can occur in any region on Earth. Every year many people die worldwide from natural disasters. To a certain extent, humans can prevent the damage. Rate the disasters below according to where you live. Can they happen to you?

1. earthquake ___

2. fire ___

3. flood ___

4. landslide ___

5. tornado ___

6. typhoon (hurricane) ___

7. lightning ___

8. tsunami __

9. volcanic eruption ___

The Scale

A. How likely is each of the natural disasters above? Rate them.

0 1 2 3 4 5 6 7 8 9 10

(not very likely) *(possible)* *(very possible)*

B. Compare your rating with a partner, and tell them whether you've ever experienced each disaster.

C. Now match the historical disasters below with their results. When done, discuss with your partners.

1. During the 2008 Afghan Blizzard, the temperatures were below -30°C. ___
2. Rats carried the virus that caused the "Black Death." ___
3. A 7.0 earthquake hit Haiti in 2010. ___
4. On 3.11.11, a tsunami destroyed a nuclear power plant in Fukushima. ___
5. It hardly rained during the 2003 European heat wave. ___
6. Hurricane Katrina destroyed houses on the U.S.'s Gulf Coast. ___
7. The "Arduous March" famine devastated North Korea. ___
8. In 1931, very heavy rains hit China. ___
9. In the 1970 "Bhola Cyclone" in Bangladesh, winds reached 185 kilometers per hour. ___
10. The Spanish flu of 1918 spread throughout Asia, Europe, and North America. ___
11. In December 2004, the 9.2 Sumatra Earthquake caused a tsunami. ___

a) starvation
b) much property damage
c) up to 200 million died on three continents
d) frostbite
e) destroyed poor villages
f) Yangtze River flood
g) many died at sea
h) many people were evacuated
i) half of all Europeans died
j) 100,000 people were crushed by buildings
k) drought

After discussing, check these answers: *1d, 2i, 3j, 4h, 5k, 6b, 7a, 8f, 9e, 10c, 11g*

Share your ratings and discuss them with your partners.

21. Thinking Deeper about
Refugees

Refugees are people forced to leave their home due to war, discrimination, or some other danger. Should your country accept refugees?

The Scale

Should your country accept the refugees below? Rate on a scale of 0 to 10.

0	1	2	3	4	5	6	7	8	9	10

(do not accept) — *(definitely accept)*

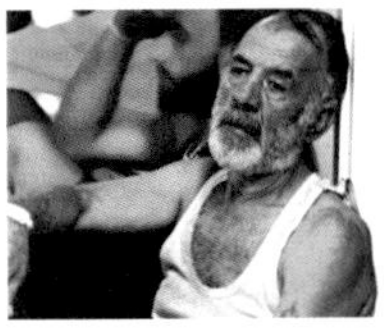

1. Ahmed (68 years old) and 8 family members escaped the war in Syria. Criminals in Libya took their money, raped the women, then sank their boat. Only Ahmed survived. __

2. Agid and Sherin are minorities, Kurds, in Syria. They escaped to Greece but can't stay permanently. After seven attempts to leave Greece, they have lost their lifetime savings and are losing hope. If they don't find a country, they will have to return to Syria, where they will surely be imprisoned and probably killed. __

3. When Aziz was 10, he saw his father killed in Afghanistan. He and his brother escaped to Iran, where they lived with no money or job for three years. Then Aziz went to Greece, where he was beaten on the street. He is heartbroken to have had his father's ring stolen, the only memory he had of his dad. He wants to leave for a safer country. __

4. Yacoub (29) and his family escaped violence in Myanmar in 2012 and went to Bangladesh. Yacoub teaches children the Koran in a village mosque, but cannot make enough money to feed his family of six. He hopes to go abroad to find work. His wife Shahina, 25, is worried, but she cannot stop him from making the dangerous journey. __

Discuss your ratings with your partners.

22. Thinking Deeper about
Human Rights

On December 10, 1948, countries from every region in the world agreed on certain rights that every citizen should have. The Declaration of Human Rights was made. Which of these rights are most important? Which do you feel most strongly about?

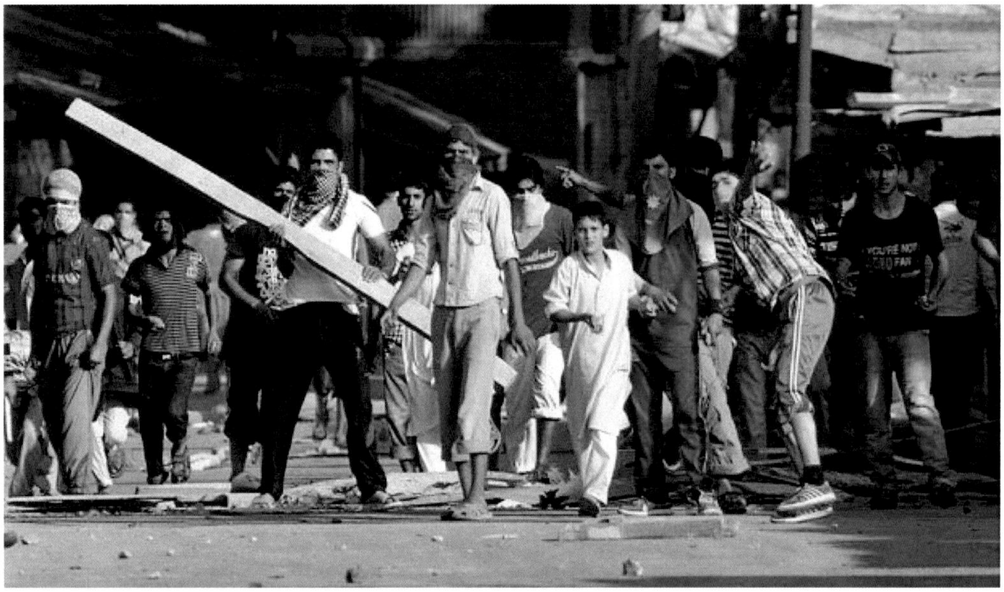

The Scale

How important is each statement listed below? Rate on a scale of 0 to 10.

0 — 1 — 2 — 3 — 4 — 5 — 6 — 7 — 8 — 9 — 10

(least important) *(medium importance)* *(most important)*

1. All human beings are born with equal rights. __
2. Everyone has the right to live free from discrimination. __
3. Everyone has the right to life, liberty, and security. __
4. All humans are free and shall never become slaves of any kind. __
5. Everyone has a right to legal counsel (a lawyer) when arrested. __
6. A person is innocent until proven guilty. __
7. If a person is facing severe discrimination or is in great danger, he or she may seek shelter in another country as a refugee. __
8. Everyone has a right to own property. __
9. Everyone has the right to meet others, and protest, peacefully. __
10. Everyone has the right to freely choose a job. __
11. Everyone has a right to an education. __
12. The Universal Declaration of Human Rights (UDHR) is a Western idea and should not be forced on other countries. __

Share your ratings and discuss them with your partners.

23. Thinking Deeper about
Political Correctness

Political correctness is language or actions that avoid offending others. For example, if a person says men and women have different needs, or people of two races are different physically, they might be criticized. The speaker, however, might feel they are just speaking honestly and accurately and their critics are demanding "political correctness." The critics, on the other hand, feel the speaker is saying something wrong or offensive. Consider the situations.

The Scale

To what extent do you agree or disagree with the actions below?

0	1	2	3	4	5	6	7	8	9	10
(strongly disagree!)					*(middle)*					*(strongly agree!)*

1. A school no longer says *Christmas tree*. Instead, they are called *holiday trees*. __
2. Many Americans now say *Happy Holidays* rather than *Merry Christmas*. __
3. Christians are upset because *Bible* and *God* don't always get capitalized these days. __
4. The EU proposed eliminating titles such as *Miss* and *Mrs.* that indicate marital status. __
5. Violence in cartoons such as *Bugs Bunny* is removed. __
6. U.S. President Trump complained about NFL athletes not standing up for the National Anthem. __
7. A non-Jew claims Jews are more intelligent than people of other races. __
8. Protestors say Washington's football team name *Redskins* should be changed because it is offensive to Native Americans. __
9. Whites angry about *Black Lives Matter* start a group called *All Lives Matter*. __
10. Students and teachers at some schools are expected to use gender-neutral terms such as *ze/zir/zirs* or *xe/xem/xyrs* instead of *him* or *her* for transgender individuals. __
11. Washington State prisons refer to *inmates* as *students*. __
12. A U.S. customer at a store is angry to see a sign written in Spanish as well as English. __
13. Every time a man disagrees with a news story he calls it "fake." __
14. A man claims women are, by nature, better than men at caring for infants. __
15. An American criticizes a boy in Japan who applies "blackface" at a Halloween party. __

Share your ratings and discuss with a partner. Is anyone being politically incorrect? Who?

24. Thinking Deeper about
Stereotypes

A stereotype is a negative and mostly false opinion of a group of people, often a nationality or gender. There might, however, be some truth to the opinions we have. Look at the pictures and decide what the stereotype is.

The Scale

How true are the stereotypes below? Rate on a scale of 0 to 10. Also, write your impressions.

0	1	2	3	4	5	6	7	8	9	10
(most untrue)					*(somewhat true)*					*(truest)*

stereotype		your impression
1. Mexicans are	lazy.	______________________
2. Italians are	romantic.	______________________
3. Germans are	severe.	______________________
4. Japanese are	shy.	______________________
5. Russians are	strong.	______________________
6. Chinese are	noisy.	______________________
7. The French are	unfriendly.	______________________
8. The British are	pessimistic.	______________________
9. Koreans are	aggressive.	______________________
10. Canadians are	friendly.	______________________
11. Americans are	ignorant.	______________________
12. Arabs are	materialistic.	______________________
13. Iranians are	paranoid.	______________________

Compare your answers with your partners and discuss your impressions.

25. Thinking Deeper about
Drugs

Drugs are substances that affect a person's mind and/or body. Many drugs are illegal, while others are legal. For example, tobacco and alcohol are legal drugs. Medicines can also be called drugs. Rate how dangerous you think the drugs below are.

The Scale

How dangerous are the drugs below? Rate them.

-10 · -8 · -6 · -4 · -2 · 0 · 2 · 4 · 6 · 8 · 10

(most dangerous) *(neither dangerous nor helpful)* *(most beneficial)*

1. Opium is made from sap of poppy plants. It is usually smoked but can be eaten. __
2. Caffeine is a stimulant in coffee, tea, and cocoa. __
3. Marijuana is from the Cannabis plant; people smoke it to feel "high." __
4. Beer and wine are types of alcohol that can get people drunk. __
5. Whiskey is a strong alcoholic beverage made from fermented grains. __
6. LSD is a man-made illegal drug that affects nerves and mood. __
7. Cocaine is a highly addictive white powder stimulant usually sniffed into the nose. __
8. "Magic mushrooms" grow naturally in forests; they help users "trip" and feel bliss. __
9. Anti-depressants like Xanax are legal drugs available from a psychiatrist. __
10. Tobacco is a plant made into cigarettes and cigars. __
11. Amphetamines are stimulants used to stay awake. __
12. Chemotherapy is a prescribed medicine for cancer patients. __
13. Ecstasy is a "party" drug that was originally made to improve depression symptoms. __
14. Peyote, which grows wild as a cactus, makes users see visions and strange scenes. __
15. The "Opioid Epidemic" includes millions addicted to pain killers. Many have died. __

Discuss your ratings with your partners.

26. Thinking Deeper about
Materialism

"Materialism" is a tendency to focus too much on material possessions. Garbage and pollution are two results of buying and consuming so many material goods. We focus so much on material goods, some say, because our lives are empty. We mistakenly think buying and owning goods will bring happiness. On the other hand, we need material goods to survive. What do you feel you need?

The Scale

Assuming you have enough money to do these things, to what extent are the actions listed below truly needed, or unnecessary (materialistic)? Rate each one.

0 — 1 — 2 — 3 — 4 — 5 — 6 — 7 — 8 — 9 — 10

(truly needed) *(somewhat needed)* *(materialistic)*

1. Purchase a second car, a sports car, for going on weekend drives. __
2. Own seven Rolls Royce luxury cars. __
3. Buy a "mystery gift bag" containing unknown items for $200. __
4. Shop for new clothes every autumn when new fashions are introduced. __
5. Buy a third bicycle, a racing bike, because it's faster than your other bikes. __
6. Buy a blender so you can make smoothies from fresh fruit and vegetables. __
7. Buy a new sofa because the one you have is starting to wear out. __
8. If you are single, buy a 12-room mansion with a huge yard. __
9. Buy five new televisions: one for each bedroom, the living room, and the guest room. __
10. Collect art, buying many paintings, more than you can hang on your walls. __
11. Buy an expensive vacation home, and stay there two or three weeks a year. __
12. Buy ten new DVDs a month. __
13. Travel to Paris for a weekend, staying at a five-star hotel with your girl/boyfriend. __
14. Buy and drink bottled water. __
15. Rent a 100-foot yacht for a weekend with your boy/girlfriend.

Discuss your answers with your partners.

25. Thinking Deeper about

Population

Many people believe the world is overpopulated. There are many ways to look at the issue. How many people is most desirable? What, if anything, can be done to keep a city population, or the global population, at a desired level?

The Scale

To what extent do you agree with the statements about population below? Rate them.

0	1	2	3	4	5	6	7	8	9	10
(not at all)		*(a little)*			*(yes and no)*		*(very much)*		*(strongly agree)*	

1. Some cities are overcrowded, but the world is not overpopulated. __
2. Overpopulation is one of the most serious problems today. __
3. There is enough food in the world for everyone. __
4. Families with more than two children should pay a fine or tax. __
5. Couples have a right to have as many children as they want, even ten or more. __
6. Only educated people should have three or more children. __
7. If a country's population is declining, the government should encourage more immigrants. __
8. Workers should be forced to retire at age 65. __
9. Nursery school should be free for parents, paid for with tax money. __
10. Within 100 years, underpopulation will be a bigger problem than overpopulation. __
11. A parent should be allowed to take one year off, with pay, when a child is born. __

See the world population clock at the following link: <http://www.poodwaddle.com>.
When finished, discuss the world population clock, and your answers above, with your partners.

28. Thinking Deeper about

Old Age and Death

Growing old is a fact of life. Every person or animal that is born eventually dies. Despite that fact, death is something we rarely think or talk about. Consider and rank the degree to which you agree with statements below about growing old and dying.

The Scale

How much do you agree with the ideas and suggestions below? Rate on a scale of 0 to 10.

0	1	2	3	4	5	6	7	8	9	10

(completely disagree) *(disagree)* *(middle)* *(agree)* *(completely agree)*

1. Although your 85-year-old grandmother can move around and is not showing signs of Alzheimer's, she finds it hard to care of herself, so she enters an "old folks' home." __
2. Your elderly father is showing signs of dementia, so you and your siblings force him to enter a nursing home against his will. __
3. Your parents, who are in their 70s, have suggested they live on the first floor of your house while you and your family live on the second floor. __
4. Your elderly father is showing early signs of Alzheimer's and plans to end his life. __
5. Your elderly mother, who is showing early signs of Alzheimer's, has asked you to assist her in committing suicide. __
6. Your 88-year-old grandfather insists on working outside in his garden even though it is extremely hot. __
7. You die at 93. Friends and family wear bright colors, talk, and laugh at your funeral. __
8. After you die, your body is cremated and your ashes are thrown into the sea. __
9. After you die, your body is buried at a cemetery. __
10. Christians believe you go to heaven after you die. __
11. Buddhists and most Hindus believe you are born again, reincarnated, after you die. __
12. After you die, you simply cease to exist. There is no heaven or rebirth. It's the end. __

When finished, discuss these beliefs with your partners.

29. Thinking Deeper about

Food

We enjoy food every day. Where does it come from? When is it healthiest? Some foods we eat might be unhealthy. Rank the foods below, and then discuss them with a partner.

The Scale

Write your ideas for healthy or unhealthy foods, and then rate those below on a scale of -10 to 10.

-10 -8 -6 -4 -2 0 2 4 6 8 10

(most unhealthy) *(medium)* *(healthiest)*

1. A soda which contains sugar, caffeine, and carbonated water. ___
2. A convenience store box lunch with fish, rice, vegetables, and a pickle. ___
3. Pork from a pig that was killed at a crowded pig farm. ___
4. Carrots grown in your grandfather's garden. ___
5. Mango imported from a tropical region and sold during winter in your country. ___
6. Fresh meat deer from a deer your friend killed while hunting in a forest. ___
7. Barley tea. ___
8. Beer. ___
9. Persimmon picked from a nearby tree. ___
10. A fried grasshopper or other insect purchased at a food stall in Laos. ___
11. A banana so ripe that it's mostly black and getting soft. ___
12. Edible wild plants such as dandelion picked in a field in the country. ___
13. Bamboo shoots harvested in spring. ___
14. Cashew nuts. ___
15. Mushrooms you found in the woods and identified in a book as edible. ___
16. Popcorn popped at home, with a little sea salt and no butter. ___
17. Peanut butter that is a month past the "Best use by" date. ___
18. "Clean meat" that was created in a laboratory. ___

Compare your answers with your partners and discuss them.

30. Thinking Deeper about

Money

"Money makes the world go around" is a famous saying. We spend a lot of time thinking about money. Our economic system and our jobs are based on money. We face tough decisions regarding what to spend our money on. Read the situations below and decide what you would do.

The Scale

How do you feel about spending money in the ways described below? Rate on a scale of 0 to 10.

0	1	2	3	4	5	6	7	8	9	10

(no way!) *(probably not)* *(maybe yes maybe no)* *(probably)* *(definitely!)*

1. At 20, you travel around the world spending most of the $1,000,000 you inherited. ___
2. At 30, you save all of the million dollars you just inherited. ___
3. You are in Egypt where shopkeepers overcharge, expecting to bargain. The carpet you want to buy is, from your point of view, cheap. You bargain for ten minutes anyway. ___
4. Your best friend lost all his money gambling. He has apparently recovered and asks you to lend him $200. Since you have the money, and like him, you lend it to him. ___
5. Your best friend's child needs an operation to save her life. She asks for $10,000. You have $50,000 saved, and have no plans to use it, but you do not lend her the money. ___
6. You find $50,000 in cash. Nobody can possibly see you, so you take it and keep it. ___
7. While abroad, you find $100 on the street. No one there trusts police, so you keep it. ___
8. You discover your friend has been stealing money from rich tourists. You also know that the same friend donates the money to orphanages, so you say nothing. ___
9. You are poor and have no savings. Every week you buy lottery tickets. ___
10. When in Las Vegas you set aside $1,000 to gamble. After losing that, you stop. ___
11. All the best things in life are free. ___

When finished, share your ratings and discuss with a partner.

31. Thinking Deeper about
Health

Staying healthy is one of our most important challenges in life. What are the most healthful activities for mind and body? Rate the activities below.

The Scale

Rate how healthy each activity is.

-10 -8 -6 -4 -2 0 2 4 6 8 10

(most unhealthy) *(medium)* *(healthiest)*

1. earn a black belt in karate ___
2. train and run in a full marathon (42.2 km) ___
3. train and run in Ironman competitions (3.86 km swim, 180.3 km bicycle ride and a 42.2 km run, in that order without a break) ___
4. lift weights intensively every other day to build strength and muscle ___
5. plant, take care of, and harvest a large vegetable garden ___
6. walk a dog for 20 minutes every morning and evening ___
7. go on a month-long bicycle trek carrying a tent, sleeping bag, food, etc. ___
8. kayak every weekend on a lake or the sea ___
9. do housework such as vacuuming and washing clothes daily ___
10. practice tai chi with a group every morning in a nearby park ___
11. attend ballroom dance classes twice a week for many years ___
12. hike up mountains on weekends ___
13. do 20 push-ups a day ___
14. do 50 sit-ups a day ___
15. practice and play Ping Pong in tournaments ___
16. travel abroad for 6 months ___
17. jog one kilometer three days a week ___
18. practice yoga postures 3 or 4 days a week ___

When finished, discuss the topic with your partners.

32. Thinking Deeper about
Happiness

We all seek happiness in life. People find happiness in many ways. What makes you happy? Rate the situations below on how much happiness they bring to you.

The Scale

To what extent would the situations below make you happy or sad? Rate them.

-10	-8	-6	-4	-2	0	2	4	6	8	10
(saddest)		*(a little sad)*		*(neither happy nor sad)*				*(happy)*		*(happiest)*

1. You are an excellent athlete. __
2. Your favorite team wins the championship. __
3. You graduate, work part-time at a convenience store, and live with your parents. __
4. You or your girlfriend gets pregnant before marriage. __
5. You find a good job but must work 12 or 13 hours a day, six days a week. __
6. You find a girl/boyfriend whom you like while secretly loving someone else more. __
7. You or your wife gives birth to your third child. __
8. You win the lottery, collecting a million dollars. __
9. You have just landed in Europe where you will begin traveling around the world. __
10. You join your country's compulsory military for two years. __
11. Your spouse dies. You (80) live alone in a city apartment but often meet friends. __
12. You've had a great career but never married or had kids. You are 80. __
13. You've only had enough money for necessities but are happily married. You are 80. __

Compare your answers and discuss them with your partners.

33. Thinking Deeper about
Emotions

Emotions are experiences with happy or sad feelings. Because of our personality and culture, we might feel some emotions are fine while others are unacceptable. Below are some situations to think about, rank, and discuss.

The Scale

What do you think about the statements below? Rate on a scale of 0 to 10.

0	1	2	3	4	5	6	7	8	9	10
(no way!)		*(I don't think so)*		*(maybe yes maybe no)*			*(I think so)*		*(absolutely!)*	

1. Crying is a sign of weakness. __
2. Boys and men should hide their tears. __
3. People should not cry in public. __
4. I feel embarrassed if I cry while watching or reading a fictional story. __
5. I minimize crying at a funeral. __
6. Politicians who cry cannot be trusted. __
7. I want others to comfort me when I cry. __
8. I am moody. __
9. I try to hide disappointment. __
10. I try to hide anger. __
11. I have recently lost my temper. __
12. My anger creates problems for me. __
13. Anger is natural, so experiencing it is no problem. __
14. Anger is harmful to a person's health. __
15. I get annoyed easily. __
16. When something annoys me, I think about it obsessively. __
17. I can control my fear. __
18. There is nothing to fear but fear itself. __
19. Everyone is afraid to die. __
20. Getting close to someone who might become my boy/girlfriend makes me nervous. __
21. It's important for humans to often touch people we love. __
22. I like to hold hands in public with my partner. __
23. We should often say "I love you" to loved ones. __
24. Saying "I love you" is unnecessary. __
25. I have loved a pet. __
26. I often laugh while watching comedy programs or movies. __
27. I often feel joy while listening to music. __
28. I often clap enthusiastically at concerts and sporting events. __
29. I shout encouragement to athletes when watching sports. __
30. I recently laughed so hard I cried. __

When finished, share your ratings and discuss with a partner.

34. Thinking deeper about

Past Cultures

While it is difficult to look beyond our cultural norms and consider foreign cultures, it is even harder when we are trying to understand cultures of the past. It is very difficult, if not impossible, to not judge from a modern perspective. Nevertheless, consider this picture and how it makes you feel.

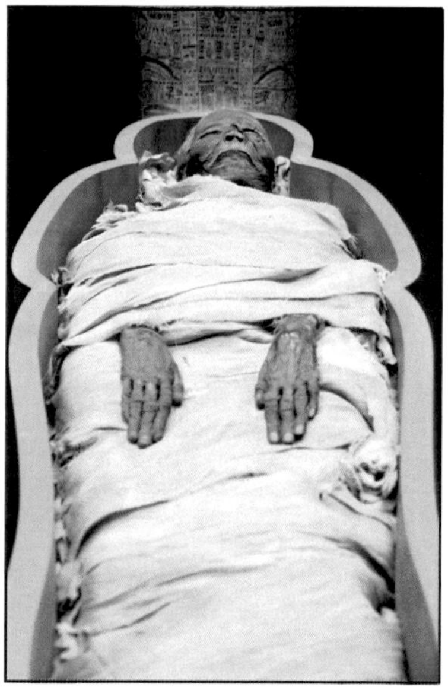

The Scale: *What do you think about the customs below? Rate on a scale of 0 to 10.*

0	1	2	3	4	5	6	7	8	9	10
(most troubling)			*(troubling)*		*(a bit troubling)*		*(questionable)*			*(fine)*

1. In ancient China, girls' feet were wrapped tightly to keep them from growing large, because men preferred women with small feet. __
2. If a guest in China expressed admiration for anything in the home (a painting, piece of furniture, etc.), the host felt obliged to give it away as a present. __
3. Marriages in China and Europe were arranged until the 20th century. The young man and woman didn't see each other until the wedding day and could not refuse. __
4. Medieval Europeans rarely bathed, because the Church thought nudity was immoral and people believed the water could cause illness. __
5. In the past, when cannibalism was practiced in Fiji, Fijian tribesmen killed and cannibalized a Christian missionary after he touched the chief on the head, a taboo. __
6. Japanese samurai would commit "seppuku," ritual suicide, to preserve honor. __
7. American women could not vote until 1920. __
8. Until 1994, blacks in South Africa were systematically discriminated against and segregated under "Apartheid." __
9. Rich Egyptians, including kings and queens, were rubbed with an herb when they died to preserve their bodies, wrapped as mummies, and buried with their favorite possessions. __
10. Aztec people would kill a child to sacrifice it to their gods. __

When finished, share your ratings and discuss with a partner.

35. Thinking deeper about

Foreign Cultures

Culture influences the way we think and the way we experience the world. Are there global standards we can apply to decide whether a custom is wise and desirable or harmful and thus should not be practiced? Rate the sentences.

The Scale: *What do you think about the customs below? Rate on a scale of 0 to 10.*

0	1	2	3	4	5	6	7	8	9	10
(should stop)			*(troubling)*		*(a bit troubling)*		*(questionable)*			*(fine)*

1. Kayan tribeswomen in Myanmar stretch their necks by putting more and more rings around them from a young age. __
2. In several countries, young girls suffer through a painful and unnecessary operation known as "FGM," female genital mutilation. __
3. When a Yanomami tribe person dies, the body is burned. The ashes are then put in a soup that other tribe members consume. __
4. Women in some Middle Eastern countries have to wear a burqa, a black cloth that covers them head to toe, whenever they leave the house. __
5. Catholics in the Philippines whip themselves bloody to show love for Christ. __
6. If fighting for a just cause (jihad), Muslims may want to become martyrs by dying for the cause, even as suicide bombers. __
7. In Spain, bulls are let loose down city streets as millions of people watch. Bulls then face matadors, costumed performers with capes, who almost always stab them to death. __
8. Young women in Mauritania, Africa, are sent to 'fat camps' where they are fed up to 15,000 calories a day because fat women are more desirable as wives. __
9. Dani women in Indonesia are forced to cut off a fingertip when their husband dies. __
10. During a festival in Yulin, China, thousands of dogs are killed and eaten along with lychee fruit. __
11. During a winter festival, Russians swim in freezing cold lake water. __
12. An Amazon rainforest tribe forces boys to be stung many times by the most powerful and painful ants, "bullet ants," in a ritual that welcomes the boys into manhood. __

When finished, share your ratings and discuss with a partner.

36. Thinking deeper about
Traveling or Living in Japan

A famous saying goes, 'When in Rome, do as the Romans do.' How strictly do customs need to be followed when traveling? In some cases, a foreigner might feel unnatural following the customs of locals. Furthermore, some citizens might not expect foreigners to keep particular customs. Rank the situations below.

The Scale: *What do you think about the situations below? Rate on a scale of 0 to 10.*

0	1	2	3	4	5	6	7	8	9	10
(should stop)			*(troubling)*		*(a bit troubling)*		*(questionable)*			*(fine)*

1. A foreigner in Japan sits on a desktop and puts his feet (with shoes on) on a chair. __
2. A foreigner in Japan doesn't bow low enough to show respect to an elderly man. __
3. A foreigner doesn't use a stamp (*hanko*). Instead, she always signs her name. __
4. A young Japanese is told by his American host to leave his shoes on in the house but the boy keeps taking off his shoes and leaving them in the foyer (*genkan*). __
5. A Thai host father tells his Japanese guest that Thai people shower three times a day. The Japanese boy gets sweaty in the afternoon but still doesn't shower. __
6. A Japanese host prepares delicious coffee but a foreigner refuses it because caffeine keeps her awake. __
7. A foreigner walks up the escalator even though Japanese are just standing. __
8. A foreigner sticks his chopsticks into his rice while eating with Japanese friends. __
9. A foreigner sticks his chopsticks into his rice while eating alone in public. __
10. A Christian foreigner visits a Shinto shrine but doesn't bow, clasp his hands (*gasho*) or give coins. __
11. Jehovah's Witnesses move to Japan to convince Japanese to join their religion. __
12. A foreign man in Japan blows his nose into a handkerchief and puts it in his pocket. __
13. A tourist does not tip a taxi driver. __
14. A foreign couple hug and kiss in a crowded mall. __

When finished, share your ratings and discuss with a partner.

37. Thinking Deeper about

Comparing Cultures: U.S. and France

Even if cultures have a significant amount of shared history, they can often be very different. The observations below were made by a French man living in America. What do you think?

The Scale

Rate how true each cultural tendency is for your country and then for yourself personally.

-10	-8	-6	-4	-2	0	2	4	6	8	10
(not true)					(medium)					(truest)

Americans	French	your country	yourself
1. are very direct	are very indirect		
2. are optimistic	are pessimistic		
3. black-white thinking	"it depends" thinking		
4. like simplicity	like complexity		
5. individualism	group is important		
6. value cleanliness	don't value cleanliness		
7. value work	value leisure / life		
8. "eat to live"	"food is life"		
9. innovation valued	tradition valued		
10. outgoing	grumpy / unsociable		

When finished, share your ratings and discuss with a partner.

38. Thinking Deeper about
Foreign Customs

Which aspects of foreign cultures do you find strange or surprising? Many of the cultural practices below might seem normal to people in that country. Read each one and consider the reasons for it and whether it is sensible and desirable.

The Scale: *What do you think about the customs below? Rate on a scale of 0 to 10.*

0 — 1 — 2 — 3 — 4 — 5 — 6 — 7 — 8 — 9 — 10

(strangest/most undesirable) *(neutral)* *(sensible/desirable)*

1. When visiting, you should always bring a gift for the host. __
2. After receiving a gift you are obliged to give a "return gift" of half value. __
3. You must always remove your shoes before entering a home. __
4. From middle school, you must intensively study many hours a day for the university entrance exam. __
5. A foreigner, not wanting to blow his nose in public, continually sniffs. __
6. There is a "Smoking" section in a restaurant even though the smell drifts into the "Non-smoking" section. __
7. Diners in a restaurant loudly slurp their noodles. __
8. Some foreigners wear a mask due to worries about their appearance. __
9. People with tattoos are not allowed in hot spring spas. __
10. Workers do not take their vacation time because they don't want to inconvenience co-workers. __
11. Workers have the same holidays, 3 days in spring and 3 for New Year's. __
12. Guns are strictly regulated; even police don't carry firearms. __
13. A comedian in Asia applies "blackface" to get laughs. __
14. When refusing an invitation, saying a vague excuse like "I have plans" is acceptable. __

When finished, share your ratings and discuss with a partner..

39. Thinking Deeper about
Educational Travel

What is your reason for traveling? To learn a language? To try different food? To meet people? One reason for traveling is learning. How educational are the trips below?

The Scale

How valuable do you think the experiences below are? Rate them.

0	1	2	3	4	5	6	7	8	9	10
(no value)					*(some value)*					*(greatest value)*

1. A man joins an "eco-tour" on the Amazon River to learn about rare plant species. ___
2. A woman takes a trip to Las Vegas with $500 to play the slot machines. ___
3. A woman travels to the Arctic to see a region of the earth untouched by humans. ___
4. A Muslim pilgrim travels to Mecca in Saudi Arabia for religious reasons. ___
5. An elderly Buddhist walks the 88 temple pilgrimage route in Shikoku. ___
6. A man visits the Hiroshima Peace Museum to learn about wars and weapons. ___
7. A woman does volunteer work at an orphanage overseas for two weeks. ___
8. A man takes a trip to Germany to spend a week at Oktoberfest. ___
9. A woman lives a year with a remote tribe in the rainforest. ___
10. A man lives for a year with the homeless to learn about their lives. ___

Share your answers with your partners. Discuss which trips appeal to you most and why.

40. Thinking Deeper about

Child-Parent Relationships

The most important early relationship most kids have is with their mother or father. What makes a strong parent-child relationship? Rate the ideas below.

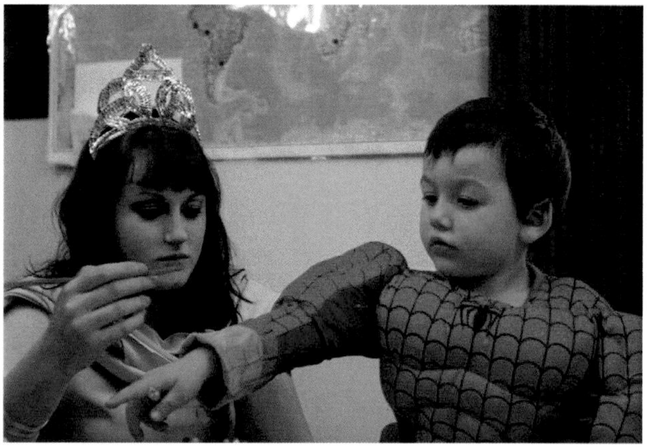

The Scale

Rate the following suggestions for getting along better with parents.

0	1	2	3	4	5	6	7	8	9	10
(worst)		(so-so)			(pretty good)			(good)		(best)

1. Children should always obey parents. __
2. Instead of expressing anger, parents should patiently explain why they are angry. __
3. Parents should make as few rules as possible. __
4. Parents shouldn't hesitate to spank or slap their children to teach them. __
5. Families should spend more time together. __
6. Youth should ask for help only when they need it. __
7. Youth should always explain their feelings, not hide them. __
8. Listen more carefully and completely to each other. __
9. Parents and children should hug each other more often. __
10. Youth should volunteer to do more household chores. __
11. Parents should not expect youth to do many household chores. __
12. Parents and children should say "I love you" more often. __
13. Youth should always try their best. __
14. Parents should lower their expectations for how their children perform in school. __
15. Parents should attend parenting workshops. __
16. Youth and parents should always be honest. __
17. Youth should always respect parents. __
18. Parents should always be excellent role models for their kids. __

When finished, discuss your ratings with your partners.

41. Thinking Deeper about
Adulthood

In the past, children entered adulthood much earlier than they do now. When should children be allowed to do actions generally reserved for adults?

From what age should children be allowed to do the following? Write the age next to the action.

1. play alone outside __
2. babysit for a little sister/brother __
3. use matches __
4. cut grass or shovel snow for money __
5. work a part-time job at a store __
6. freely surf the internet __
7. become a parent __
8. get a credit card __
9. vote in an election __
10. shoot a gun __
11. get a hunting license __
12. get a driving license __
13. receive an allowance __
14. not be allowed to sleep with parents __
15. not be allowed to bathe with parents __
16. not be allowed naked on a beach __
17. sleep overnight at a friend's house __
18. stay out until midnight __
19. travel alone on trains __
20. travel abroad alone __
21. sip a little alcohol at home __
22. drink alcohol outside home __
23. decide school subjects to study __
24. quit school __
25. be left alone overnight __
26. register for Facebook __
27. cook dinner without supervision __
28. bungee jump __
29. smoke cigarettes __
30. smoke marijuana __
31. live alone __
32. go on a date __
33. get married without permission __
34. join the army __

When finished, tell your partners what you wrote. Also, tell whether you have experienced any of these activities and, if so, at what age.

42. Thinking Deeper about
Household Chores

Household chores have to be done to keep a home running smoothly. Which chores should children and teenagers do?

The Scale

How often should a teenager be expected to do each of the household chores below?

0	1	2	3	4	5	6	7	8	9	10
(never)		*(occasionally)*			*(sometimes)*		*(often)*			*(always)*

1. take out the trash __
2. wash the dishes __
3. set the table __
4. wash their own clothes __
5. buy food at the market __
6. cook their own breakfast __
7. make their lunch for school __
8. make their own dinner __
9. paint the house __
10. work on the family farm __
11. take the family dog for a walk __
12. feed the cat __
13. wash the car __
14. shovel snow __
15. cut grass __

When finished, compare your answers with your partners'. Also, tell about your experiences as a child doing household chores.

43. Thinking Deeper about
Work Benefits

Most people have to work to survive. Some people get rich at their jobs. Others work long, hard hours for low pay. How much do workers deserve? What about benefits?

Are teachers underpaid?

Do hair stylists make enough money?

The Chart

Imagine a 24-year-old worker working at each occupation below. What salary and benefits do they deserve?

	factory worker	teacher	doctor	company manager	head cook	pro athlete	your idea
1. monthly salary (or)	ex. No						
2. hourly wage	ex. about $11/hour						
3. overtime rate	ex. "time and a half"						
4. working hours	ex. 30 flexible hours/week						
5. vacation	ex. six weeks/year						
6. health insurance	ex. Yes						
7. paid extra for training	ex. No						
8. uniform/ how many	ex. Yes, two						

Discuss your answers with your partners.

44. Thinking Deeper about
Ethical Dilemmas I

Ethics refers to the degree to which a person's conduct follows society's rules. Individuals have different ways to think about ethics. What seems certainly wrong to one person might be fine in another person's eyes. Rate each situation below.

The Scale

How ethical or unethical is each situation below? Rate on a scale of 0 to 10.

0	1	2	3	4	5	6	7	8	9	10
(unethical)		*(quite unethical)*			*(a little unethical)*		*(questionable)*			*(ethical)*

1. You think your friend's new hairstyle looks bad but tell her it looks great. __
2. You are required to take an English course but have no interest. So you cheat on tests. __
3. After finding a wallet with $50 you return the wallet in the post but keep the cash. __
4. After a year of using pirated software for free, you pay for it. __
5. You can no longer care for your pet cat, so you leave it in a park. __
6. You rescue a puppy but don't pay to "fix" it with surgery. Thus, it can have puppies. __
7. When you don't have anything to do at work, you send private email messages. __
8. After noticing that the cashier gave you $1 extra change, you say nothing. __
9. You find $80,000 in cash. Nobody can possibly see you, so you take it and keep it. __
10. When a homeless man asks for spare change on the street, you refuse. __
11. You tell the box office your son is nine so he gets a discount, but he is actually ten. __
12. You torture an enemy soldier because you believe he knows about a terrorist attack. __
13. The day before your wedding, you make out with an ex, thinking it's your last chance. __
14. You have an affair because your relationship with your spouse is very bad. __
15. To get insurance money, you pretend your car got damaged in a typhoon. __
16. You spread lies about a politician because his policies are causing great damage. __
17. You don't repay a friend, because they lost your favorite CD the previous year. __
18. You set traps that kill crows because they are eating your garden vegetables. __

Write your own ethical dilemma if time allows. Share it and your ratings and discuss with a partner.

45. Thinking Deeper about
Ethical Dilemmas II

Ethics are the principles or ideas that guide our behavior. We receive our ethical training from our parents, teachers, and societies. While most individuals can agree on principles such as "Do not kill," many situations arise that are tougher to judge. Be the judge below.

The Scale

What do you think about the statements below? Rate on a scale of 0 to 10.

0	1	2	3	4	5	6	7	8	9	10
(most unethical)			*(unethical)*		*(middle)*		*(a little dodgy)*			*(most ethical)*

1. Your married boss asks you out on a date. You agree to go to discuss the situation. __
2. A woman frequently watches movies she downloaded on a "free movie" website. __
3. A part-time university teacher feels his university employer is taking advantage of him, so he starts his 90-minute classes 15 minutes late and ends them 20 minutes early. __
4. A wife hides money from a part-time job, saving it to buy herself nice things. __
5. A man cuts down and takes a tree from a privately owned forest. __
6. A man steals rare, expensive medicine to save his wife. __
7. A woman joins an online course. She tries to drop the course but can't because the deadline has passed. When the university bills her $1,500, she quits and never pays. __
8. A foreigner who finishes her three-year contract lies, telling her university she will return to her home country so she can collect $3,000 for a return ticket. __
9. Two patients urgently need organ transplants. None are available. Another patient dies. The doctor uses their organs (with permission) to save the others. __
10. A high schooler is looking at his phone while bicycling, so you purposely don't get out of the way and get knocked down. You claim your cell phone broke, even though it had been broken before. The bicyclist's parents pay you for a new cell phone. __
11. When selling your car, you don't tell about a possible problem. __

Share your ratings, and discuss them with your partners.

46. Thinking Deeper about

Morality I

Morals refers to a person's sense of right and wrong. Morality, as opposed to ethics, is often used in a religious sense. How immoral, if at all, are the actions below? Rate each situation below.

The Scale

How immoral is each situation below? Rate on a scale of 0 to 10.

0	1	2	3	4	5	6	7	8	9	10
(no problem)		*(questionable)*		*(a little immoral)*			*(immoral)*		*(most immoral)*	

Kevin	
As an 8-year-old, Kevin keeps pulling a cat's tail to annoy it.	
In junior high school, Kevin often lies to his mother, brother, and teacher.	
In high school, Kevin takes his father's *Playboy*, a pornographic magazine, and looks at it with classmates.	
In high school, Kevin cheats on all his Spanish tests.	
In college, Kevin regularly smokes marijuana, and sometimes takes stronger drugs, like LSD.	
In his 30s, Kevin has an affair with his friend's wife.	
Kevin joins the army because he needs money, gets sent to a war, and kills an enemy soldier.	
In his 50s, Kevin keeps borrowing from his elderly parents with no intention to pay them back.	
TOTAL	

David	
As a child, David kills ants, spiders, beetles, butterflies, and worms, for no reason.	
While bullying a boy, David broke the boy's arm. David feels bad because he didn't intend to hurt the boy physically.	
David steals candy from the teacher's desk and shares it with classmates.	
After attending church every week with his family throughout his youth, David stops going and becomes an atheist.	
The third time he notices an electronic dictionary left in his university classroom, he takes it home and keeps it.	
David often uses words like *hell* and *damn*.	
David abandons his pet cat because he thinks he might be allergic to it.	
As a 48-year-old company worker, David notices that his company is polluting a river with dangerous chemicals, but says nothing.	
TOTAL	

When finished, share your ratings and discuss with a partner.

47. Thinking Deeper about

Morality II

Rate these acts by giving each a score from 0 (no problem), to 10 (the most immoral), then add the scores. Later, discuss your answers and scores with a partner.

Larry	
As a teen, Larry spray-paints graffiti on buildings.	
Feeling rejected by his female high school classmates, Larry makes up rumors about girls and calls them terrible names behind their backs.	
In college, Larry becomes addicted to cocaine and spends the next year lying and stealing to support his addiction.	
In his 20s, he joins a cult. With other members he begs on the street, gives all the money to the rich leader, and has "free sex" with female cult members, who are told it is their "duty" to have sex any time a male cult member wants.	
Larry sits in "priority" train seats and never offers his seat to elderly, pregnant, nursing mothers, physically challenged, etc.	
He tries homosexuality and lives with his boyfriend for a year.	
Even though Larry is physically able to work, he claims sickness to collect unemployment insurance for a year because the insurance is nearly as much as a paycheck would be.	
TOTAL	

Phil	
At 14, Phil hits a bus with a snowball. This causes an accident in which no one is injured.	
From 18 to 23 years old, he often cheats on his girlfriends.	
When Phil marries at 25, he promises 5 years of commitment, not forever. After 5 years he falls in love with another woman. His wife won't agree to letting him have an affair, so he divorces her and remarries.	
When his four-year-old son keeps crying loudly in public, Phil slaps his face.	
While a soldier, Phil refuses orders to fight in a war for two reasons: he doesn't believe the war is just and also is afraid of being killed.	
While he is still repaying a huge loan he took out on a house while living abroad, a natural disaster destroys his house. The insurance company refuses to pay, even though he thinks it should. Deeply in debt, he moves to Guatemala to avoid repaying the loan and starts over again.	
Although Phil's elderly parents ask to live with him, and he has the time and space, he refuses, forcing them to live in an "old folks' home" instead. He rarely visits them. They are heartbroken and die six months	
TOTAL	

When finished, share your ratings and discuss with a partner.

48. Thinking Deeper about

Hostage Dilemmas

Social scientists and philosophers developed questions about imagined situations to determine some aspects of our values. One situation imagined a runaway trolley; you have to control it. The brakes are broken. It is about to kill people. You, as a worker, can change the tracks, deciding who will be saved and who will die. The situation below gives you two choices. It's a dilemma. Neither is good. What will you choose. And why?

The Scale

Here is your desperate situation and twelve bad dilemmas. Choose 1 or 2 for each.

Your situation: While you are traveling abroad, rebels take 24 hostages, including you. If you do as they say, you will be released. If you refuse, you and all the other hostages will be tortured and killed. They order you to kill...

1. (1) a 50-year-old man dying of cancer or (2) three cats. __
2. (1) ten village dogs or (2) a 95-year-old man. __
3. (1) three men in their 80s, (2) a man in his 30s. __
4. (1) a 24-year-old father or (2) a 64-year-old grandmother. __
5. (1) a 28-year-old pregnant woman, (2) a same-aged single woman. __
6. (1) one child, (2) a 40-year-old doctor. __
7. (1) eight homeless people, (2) four doctors. __
8. (1) eight single men and women in their 40s, (2) four parents in their 40s. __
9. (1) four criminals, (2) one man and one woman (same age as criminals). __
10. (1) two friends of yours, (2) ten people you don't know. __
11. (1) an elderly man with terminal cancer, (2) yourself who is 30. __
12. (1) two prisoners with extreme mental illnesses, (2) a healthy prisoner. __

Explain the dilemma and discuss your choices with a partner. If you don't agree, why not?

49. Thinking Deeper about
Proverbs and Sayings

Proverbs and sayings are observations and advice about how to live. What proverbs do you know in English? What do you think about them? Rate the proverbs below.

The Scale

How wise or unwise is each proverb below? Rate on a scale of 0 to 10.

0	1	2	3	4	5	6	7	8	9	10
(unwise)					*(useful)*					*(wisest)*

1. What you don't know won't hurt you. __
2. Ignorance is bliss. __
3. Knowledge is power. __
4. Two wrongs don't make a right. __
5. When in Rome, do as the Romans do. __
6. No man is an island. __
7. The pen is mightier than the sword. __
8. Fortune favors the bold. __
9. Birds of a feather flock together. __
10. Don't bite the hand that feeds you. __
11. There's no such thing as a free lunch. __
12. Beauty is in the eye of the beholder. __
13. The early bird catches the worm. __
14. A watched pot never boils. __
15. If it ain't broke, don't fix it. __
16. Absence makes the heart grow fonder. __
17. You can't judge a book by its cover. __
18. All good things must come to an end. __

Share your ratings and discuss them with your partners.

50. Thinking Deeper about
Domestic and Tamed Animals

Some animals have gained a special status with humans as pets. Others entertain or amuse us. How should we treat animals? Some people suggest animals have many of the same rights as humans. Discuss your experiences with pets, and then rate the situations below.

The Scale

How well are owners taking care of pets in the situations below? Rate on a scale of 0 to 10.

0	1	2	3	4	5	6	7	8	9	10
(most unethical)			*(unethical)*		*(questionable)*		*(a little unethical)*			*(ethical)*

1. A group of men keep dogs for dog-fighting competitions. __
2. Except for two 20-minute walks, a dog is kept on a long chain all day every day. __
3. A dog stays inside at night. During the day, except for two 15-minute walks, the dog is kept tied to a chain. __
4. A cat is well cared for but never leaves a small apartment. __
5. A man keeps one guinea pig even though it is a social animal. __
6. A family keeps a single goldfish in a small bowl. __
7. A family keeps a bird in a small cage. It is fed but never leaves the cage. __
8. A person buys a four-week-old puppy, which is then separated from its mother. __
9. A cat, which is allowed to run freely outside all day, kills many birds. __
10. Lions and tigers are forced to perform in a circus. __
11. Dolphins are trained to perform by jumping through hoops. __
12. Fishermen capture many dolphins in the sea and sell them to aquariums. __
13. A woman keeps a turtle as a pet and feeds it living goldfish. __
14. A family finds a baby deer in the forest and keeps it as a pet in their spacious yard. __
15. A man finds a bird with a broken wing and kills it out of mercy. __
16. Hens in an unheated coop in a cold climate are kept for eggs and later for meat. __
17. A boy buys a lizard but his mother won't let him keep it inside. It dies in 0° cold. __

When finished, share your ratings and discuss with a partner.

51. Thinking Deeper about
Education

Almost every child experiences school. What sort of subjects should they study in school? Discuss the picture, and then rate each subject at various levels below.

The Scale

How important is each of the subjects below? Rate them.

0	1	2	3	4	5	6	7	8	9	10
(no value)					*(medium)*					*(greatest value)*

Early Childhood

arithmetic ___
spelling ___
reading ___
writing ___
art ___
music ___
computer science ___
ethics ___

High School

geometry ___
physics ___
history ___
English ___
a foreign language ___
cooking ___
physical education ___
government/civics ___

University

critical thinking ___
biology ___
psychology ___
sociology ___
English composition ___
world history ___
calculus ___
diversity ___ (helps students develop an understanding of the complexities of living in diverse and interconnected societies)
freshman orientation __ (helps freshmen learn basic academic skills, the school rules, how to manage time, stay out of trouble, etc.)

Discuss each subject above with a partner. Which do you think or most and least useful? Why?

52. Thinking Deeper about
A Meaningful Life

Historically, most humans did not worry about the meaning of their lives. They were too busy worrying about where to find food and how to survive. The modern world has made survival relatively easy. Now we can ask, 'Why are we here?' and 'What is a meaningful life?'

The Scale

How much do you agree with the statements about meaning below? Rate on a scale of 0 to 10.

0	1	2	3	4	5	6	7	8	9	10
(no meaning)		*(somewhat)*			*(middle)*		*(quite)*		*(most meaningful)*	

1. Enjoy delicious food and get lots of sleep. __
2. Find a job you love, one that makes a contribution to the world, and dedicate yourself to it. __
3. Become well known in your field, so colleagues respect you and go to you for advice. __
4. Become a performer, an actor, musician, comedian, etc. who entertains and is loved. __
5. Find one partner, dedicate yourself to him or her, and stay together until death. __
6. Enjoy romantic encounters with many different men or women. __
7. Become rich so you can own many possessions: artwork, cars, boats, electronics, etc. __
8. Faithfully do your duty as a child, parent, worker, community member, and citizen. __
9. Have children, raise them well, and make sure they become happy adults. __
10. Find a hobby you are passionate about, like bicycling, playing chess, drawing, etc. __
11. Try extreme challenges like climbing high mountains, rafting dangerous rivers, etc. __
12. Never stop learning: languages, technology, science, history, etc. __
13. Like other animals, survive by finding food and shelter and reproducing. __
14. Develop spiritually to become wise, compassionate, kind, etc. __
15. Life has no meaning. Doing anything, or not doing anything, is equally good. It doesn't matter. __

When finished, discuss your thoughts with your partners.

53. Thinking Deeper about
Mysteries

While science continues to broaden and deepen human knowledge, some unexplained phenomena remain. Some may be skeptical of anything labeled mysterious, completely confident there is a perfectly logical explanation. Others are convinced our beliefs and knowledge are extremely limited, and hence, anything is possible. Answer the questions below.

The Scale: *What do you think about the ideas and questions below? Rate on a scale of 0 to 10.*

0	1	2	3	4	5	6	7	8	9	10
(no way!)		*(probably not)*		*(maybe yes maybe no)*			*(probably)*		*(definitely!)*	

1. In 1986, the crew on Japan Airlines flight 1628 saw three UFOs; Captain Terauchi said he could feel the heat of the UFO on his face. All three suddenly disappeared, rising vertically. Did Captain Terauchi and his crew witness alien spacecraft? __
2. There have been many sightings of the Loch Ness monster, some with photos and videos. Does Nessie exist as an unknown animal, a dinosaur, or a monster? __
3. Stonehenge is a unique structure due to big rocks that stand atop one another. No one knows why it was created. Was it a sacred site, like a church, to heal ancient people? __
4. Plato talked about a land named Atlantis that existed in the Atlantic Ocean. He said Atlantis conquered Europe and Africa in prehistoric times. In the story, Greeks fight a conflict that ends with Atlantis disappearing in the sea. Did Atlantis exist? __
5. Bigfoot is said to be a creature that lives in the mountainous regions of North America, while rumors in Nepal talk of a similar creature, Yeti. Does either Bigfoot or Yeti exist? __
6. In 1963, President John F. Kennedy was shot by Lee Harvey Oswald. Two days later, Oswald was killed by Jack Ruby. Ruby died of lung cancer in 1967. Are there significant secrets about Kennedy's assassination that the public is unaware of? __
7. When Arthur Flowerdew saw a BBC documentary about Petra, Jordan, he recognized it and traveled there with historians. He explained many aspects of ancient life there, convincing the historians that he was reincarnated. Did Flowerdew reincarnate? __
8. The Nazca civilization created fascinating geoglyphs. These shapes, viewable from the sky, include spiders, sharks, and flowers. The details are incredible, especially since ancient people couldn't see from the sky. Is there a supernatural explanation for this? __

When finished, share your ratings and discuss with a partner.

54. Thinking Deeper about

Taboos

From childhood, there are many things we are not supposed to do. Some of these topics or actions are taboos. All cultures have topics and actions that are supposed to be avoided. Do you accept or reject the taboos described below?

The Scale: *What do you think about the taboos below? Rate on a scale of 0 to 10.*

0	1	2	3	4	5	6	7	8	9	10

(no way!) *(probably not)* *(maybe yes maybe no)* *(probably)* *(definitely!)*

Would you...

1. discuss religion on your first date with a man/woman? __
2. get a tattoo on a hidden place like your foot or back? __
3. get a tattoo on a highly visible place like your forearm or neck? __
4. eat a rice ball while sitting on a train? __
5. eat horse meat? __
6. marry a Muslim man/woman? __
7. adopt a child if you couldn't have one of your own? __
8. have sex with your cousin if you really loved him/her? __
9. try homosexuality if you really liked a gay person and she/he asked you to? __
10. leave your chopsticks stuck in your rice in a foreign country? __
11. eat an insect or worm if your host offered you some? __
12. eat dog meat if a person offered you some in a place where that was acceptable? __
13. eat human meat if you were starving and trapped on a mountain after a plane crash? __
14. drink beer with a friend at 8 a.m. on a train? __
15. rat (squeal) on your friend if they were cheating on their wife/husband? __
16. blow the whistle on your friend/coworker if they were stealing from your company? __
17. use vulgar language around your parents and grandparents? __
18. quietly burp after a big meal your host prepared for you? __
19. quietly (but not silently) pass gas (fart) with some friends in a park? __
20. talk about disgusting things like pee, constipation, or poop with a group of friends? __
21. dye your hair orange, purple, or some other unnatural color? __

When finished, share your ratings and discuss with a partner.

55. Thinking Deeper about

Nudity

The human body, like the bodies of all creatures, is perfectly natural. However, since humans started wearing clothes, seeing others naked and being seen naked, have often been thought to be shameful or taboo. In which situations is nudity somewhat or completely acceptable?

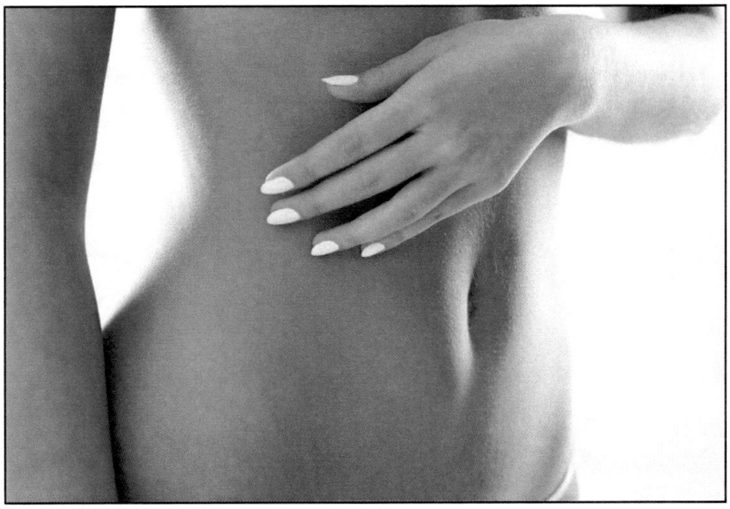

The Scale: *What do you think about the situations below? Rate on a scale of 0 to 10.*

0 1 2 3 4 5 6 7 8 9 10

(most uncomfortable) (somewhat) (middle) (mostly okay) (no problem!)

1. Your friends see baby pictures of you nude. __
2. You see many men in a foreign country walk the streets topless. __
3. You see topless women on the streets of a foreign country. __
4. Your art teacher brings a nude female model to class for students to draw. __
5. You get a part-time job as a nude model for art classes. __
6. You are nude at a same-sex hot spring spa. __
7. You are nude at a mixed-bathing hot spring spa. __
8. You are nude in front of your boy/girlfriend. __
9. You are nude with your mother in a large hot spring spa for families. __
10. You are nude with your father in a large hot spring spa for families. __
11. You are nude with your male and female colleagues at a spa. __
12. Your girl/boyfriend wants to share a few nude pictures of you with his/her friends. __
13. You are topless at a beach in Thailand. Many men and a few women are topless too. __
14. You are nude at a nude beach. Almost everyone is completely naked. __
15. While hiking, you encounter a group of nudists. All 50 people are completely naked. __
16. While you are a guest, the male host walks across the living room naked. __
17. While you are a guest, the female host walks across the living room naked. __
18. Laws are changed to legalize public nudity. __

When finished, share your ratings and discuss with a partner.

56. Thinking Deeper about

Alternative Medicine

Before regular medicine is sold it is tested extensively. Drug manufacturers have to make sure it is safe and effective. There are, however, other medicines that people take to get well. These ways may be ancient or modern. How effective do you think alternative medicines and treatments are?

The Scale: *Would you try the alternative methods below? Rate on a scale of 0 to 10.*

0	1	2	3	4	5	6	7	8	9	10
(no way!)		*(probably not)*		*(maybe yes maybe no)*			*(probably)*		*(definitely!)*	

1. An acupuncturist sticks needles in your body at pressure points to help *chi* (life force, energy) flow. __
2. A moxibustion doctor burns herbs on key points on your skin to help energy flow. __
3. People of faith pray for a sick person. __
4. You take Chinese, Indian, or Western herbs to strengthen your immune system. __
5. Homeopathy medicine is said to be the essence of an herb. The actual content of the herb is tiny, but it is said to contain the most effective part of the healing herb, its essence. __
6. Reiki was developed in Japan for stress reduction, relaxation, and healing. A Reiki healer puts her hands over a patient without necessarily touching. Reiki is based on the idea that a healer can transfer chi or positively affect the chi energy of another. __
7. A chiropractor heals patients, usually for back pain, by aligning their joints. This treatment often causes bones to make cracking sounds and can feel good. __
8. People can overcome disease and illness with the power of their mind, either by thinking positively or practicing meditation to gain power. __
9. Visualizations are images made in our minds. For example, if a man has cancer he can clearly imagine his immune system fighting and killing the cancerous cells. __
10. Dietary supplements add vitamins and minerals that we might be lacking. __

When finished, share your ratings and discuss with a partner.

57. Thinking Deeper about
Inventions

Throughout history inventions have played an important role in human evolution and culture. Modern inventions make life more enjoyable and convenient. How important was each of the inventions below?

The Scale

How useful is each of the inventions below? Rate them.

0 1 2 3 4 5 6 7 8 9 10

(totally useless) *(medium)* *(most useful)*

1. the ability to control and start fire __
2. the wheel __
3. money __
4. clocks __
5. the steam engine __
6. telescopes __
7. eyeglasses __
8. the radio __
9. electricity __
10. washing machines __
11. dishwashers __
12. karaoke __
13. disposable chopsticks __
14. nuclear power __
15. the printing press __
16. instant ramen __
17. vaccinations __
18. computers __
19. cosmetics __
20. disposable diapers __
21. eyeglasses __
22. Facebook __
23. neckties __
24. refrigerators __
25. Rubik's cube __
26. umbrellas __
27. the microwave oven __
28. vending machines __
29. GPS __
30. helicopter __
31. jet aircraft __
32. 3D printers __

When finished, share your ratings and discuss with a partner.

58. Thinking Deeper about

Future Technology

Technology began in ancient times when humans learned to control fire. Modern lives are filled with the influence of technology. What are some technological advances that humans should most actively pursue? Rate the importance of the technological inventions below.

Tiny robots to assist red blood cells could make humans healthier in the future

The Scale

How desirable are the futuristic technological developments below? Rate on a scale of 0 to 10.

0	1	2	3	4	5	6	7	8	9	10
(not desirable)			*(a little)*		*(medium)*		*(very)*			*(most desirable)*

1. Drones that will deliver packages __
2. A train or "hyperloop" that travels 1,230 kilometers per hour __
3. A machine that turns used coffee grounds into biofuel __
4. A drone that can make loud sounds to put out forest fires __
5. AI (artificial intelligence) that can create new, abstract theories such as how a flatworm regrows lost body parts __
6. A "space balloon" that takes tourists 32km above Earth into the stratosphere __
7. Viagra for women that will improve their sexual desire __
8. Cars that monitor how much alcohol a driver drank and stop drunks from driving __
9. New antibiotics harvested from the ocean __
10. The creation of 4,000 satellites that would make a high-speed wireless internet connection available to everyone on Earth __
11. A park that contains living dinosaurs and other extinct animals and plants __
12. head transplants for paralyzed patients and other severely injured individuals __

When finished, share your ratings and discuss with a partner.

59. Thinking Deeper about
Science

Science is a relatively new human endeavor. When thinkers such as Galileo began using observation and measurement, modern science was born. The advances in the past centuries, and especially the past decades, have been amazing. Some theories are unproven and may be difficult to accept.

The Scale

How much do you agree with the theories below? Rate on a scale of 0 to 10.

0	1	2	3	4	5	6	7	8	9	10

(unbelievable) (somewhat unbelievable) (middle) (quite possible) (surely true)

1. The universe will keep expanding. All the stars will burn out and everything will die. No new universe will ever be created. __
2. The universe will stop expanding, then contract, the reverse of the Big Bang. Eventually, everything in the universe will collapse into a tiny dot and later be "born" again. __
3. Instead of a "universe," one huge place for everything, we live in a "multiverse" and our universe is one among many. __
4. When scientists shake an electron it causes another electron that is millions of light years away to shake at that exact moment. This means that when two electrons are created together they are forever connected–entangled–no matter where they are. __
5. The Double Slit Experiment shows that an electron fired at a wall with two holes will sometimes go through one hole, sometimes through the other, and sometimes it will go through both holes simultaneously. This means a single electron can be in two places at one time. __
6. The Copenhagen Interpretation says all particles exist as waves of probability. That is, objects of our world only exist as probabilities, not as absolute material objects. __
7. Theories of particles, physics, do not agree with theories of space, astronomy. Einstein searched but couldn't find a "Grand Unifying Theory" that can mathematically explain everything in the universe. Such a theory exists and scientists will find it. __

When finished, discuss these ideas with your partners.

60. Thinking Deeper about
Philosophy

Throughout history people have taken time to consider life's deepest questions. Why are we humans here on Earth now? What is the meaning of life? Below are some philosophical ideas about life.

The Scale

How much do you agree with the philosophies below? Rate on a scale of 0 to 10.

0 1 2 3 4 5 6 7 8 9 10

(completely disagree) (disagree) (middle) (agree) (completely agree)

1. Some say the Big Bang must have had a cause. The only possible cause, they claim, is God. Therefore, God exists. __
2. Humans have free will. We freely make decisions. __
3. Everything has been decided. Our lives are entirely determined by fate. __
4. After we die, we will be reincarnated. If we are good, we will enjoy a comfortable birth as a wealthy human; if we are bad, we may be reborn as a frog, dog, or cockroach. __
5. Time does not exist. Things change, but humans invented time to measure changes. __
6. Plato claimed that, in addition to our world, there's another world of perfect "forms." All things we see around us are just shadows, imitations of the real things. __
7. Numbers are not just ideas but actually exist at locations in the universe. __
8. The world I experience is exactly the same as the world you experience. __
9. After the universe ends, another Big Bang will happen and the universe will be created again. This will repeat itself for eternity. __
10. "Who am I?" might be the oldest philosophical question. Some believe each person has a spiritual identity, a soul, that is eternal and can exist independent of the body. __
11. Considering another answer to "Who am I?", some believe the self does not exist. The psychological "I" is just an illusion. __

When finished, share your ratings and discuss with a partner.

Bonus! Thinking Deeper about

The Future

The 21st century is a fascinating time to be alive. Certain aspects of life, like those related to technology, are changing rapidly. In fact, technological changes are happening at a faster and faster pace. Changes are happening so fast, it is hard to imagine what the world will look like in just 50 or 100 years. Below are some predictions. What do you think of them?

The Scale

What do you think about the predictions below? Rate on a scale of 0 to 10.

0	1	2	3	4	5	6	7	8	9	10
(no way!)		*(probably not)*		*(maybe yes, maybe no)*			*(probably)*		*(definitely!)*	

1. By 2030, self-driving cars will be so common that people won't drive on highways. __
2. By the 2030s, virtual reality will feel 100% real. __
3. By 2040, 50 million people will die from a new disease. __
4. By 2045, nanobots will be put into bodies to cure most diseases. __
5. Humans will colonize Mars by 2050. __
6. By 2050, poverty will end. __
7. By 2050, overpopulation will lead to chaos and wars. __
8. By 2050, everyone will be provided a basic income and will not have to work. __
9. By 2060, humans can get all nutrition from nanobots and will no longer have to eat. __
10. By 2070, we will be able to upload our mind/consciousness and save or share it. __
11. By 2080, humans will, except due to terrible accidents, no longer die. __
12. By 2090, alien life will be confirmed, either here on Earth or on some other planet. __
13. By 2100, nanotech devices will be able to create any object out of the air on demand. __
14. By 2500, the earth will be too hot to survive due to climate change. __
15. By 3000, humans will colonize planets outside the Milky Way. __
16. By 5000, humans will be like gods, all-knowing, enlightened, with eternal life. __

How old would you like to live until? 70? 100? Forever? What changes will you see in your life?

Critical Thinking Full Checklist

Below is the full list of 35 strategies listed under ***"Dimensions of Critical Thought"*** *as explained by* **The Foundation for Critical Thinking**. *Answer "yes" or "no" for whether you did the strategy.*

Did you...

A. Affective Strategies

1. think independently? **yes no**
2. consider your own bias? **yes no**
3. consider the issue fairly? **yes no**
4. explore why you think and feel the way you do? **yes no**
5. develop intellectual humility and suspend judgment? **yes no**
6. develop intellectual courage? **yes no**
7. demonstrate integrity in your thoughts and discussions? **yes no**
8. develop perseverance? **yes no**
9. develop confidence? **yes no**

B. Cognitive Strategies (Macro-Abilities)

10. avoid generalizations and oversimplifications? **yes no**
11. compare similar situations? **yes no**
12. explore beliefs, arguments, or theories? **yes no**
13. clarify issues, conclusions, or beliefs? **yes no**
14. clarify and analyze the meanings of words or phrases? **yes no**
15. clarify values and standards? **yes no**
16. evaluate the credibility of sources of information? **yes no**
17. question deeply by considering significant questions? **yes no**
18. analyze or evaluate arguments, interpretations, beliefs, or theories? **yes no**
19. consider and assess solutions? **yes no**
20. analyze or evaluate actions or policies? **yes no**
21. read critically? **yes no**
22. listen critically? **yes no**
23. make interdisciplinary connections? **yes no**
24. clarify and question beliefs, theories, or perspectives? **yes no**
25. compare perspectives, interpretations, or theories? **yes no**
26. evaluate perspectives, interpretations, or theories? **yes no**

C. Cognitive Strategies (Micro-Skills)

27. compare and contrast ideals with actual practice? **yes no**
28. think precisely about thinking? **yes no**
29. note significant similarities and differences? **yes no**
30. examine or evaluate assumptions? **yes no**
31. distinguish relevant from irrelevant facts? **yes no**
32. make good predictions or interpretations? **yes no**
33. give reasons and evaluate evidence? **yes no**
34. recognize contradictions? **yes no**
35. explore implications and consequences? **yes no**

Survey Form

Choose five of the discussion points from each critical thinking activity. Then write how much support your classmates gave each point. See the full explanation of how to use the surveys on page vi in the Users Guide.

	(0-3) (weak or no support)	(4-6) (medium support)	(7-10) (strong support)
	______ **Survey**		
1. ______	___	___	___
2. ______	___	___	___
3. ______	___	___	___
4. ______	___	___	___
5. ______	___	___	___
	______ **Survey**		
1. ______	___	___	___
2. ______	___	___	___
3. ______	___	___	___
4. ______	___	___	___
5. ______	___	___	___
	______ **Survey**		
1. ______	___	___	___
2. ______	___	___	___
3. ______	___	___	___
4. ______	___	___	___
5. ______	___	___	___
	______ **Survey**		
1. ______	___	___	___
2. ______	___	___	___
3. ______	___	___	___
4. ______	___	___	___
5. ______	___	___	___
	______ **Survey**		
1. ______	___	___	___
2. ______	___	___	___
3. ______	___	___	___
4. ______	___	___	___
5. ______	___	___	___

Your teacher will provide more survey forms as needed.

Other Books

EFL/ESL teacher resources and textbooks for developing discussion skills from Pro Lingua Associates:

Discussion Strategies by David Kehe and Peggy Dustin Kehe
Conversation Strategies by David Kehe and Peggy Dustin Kehe
Cultural Differences by David Kehe and Peggy Dustin Kehe
Business Communication Strategies by Scott Smith
Verdicts by Jack Miller and Ray Clark
Clue by Clue by Walton Burns
Conversation Inspirations by Nancy Ellen Zelman
Surveys for Conversation by Deborah F. Hitsky
In My Opinion by Phil Keegan
Ask and Task by Nancy Ellen Zelman
Dictations for Discussion by Judy deFilippo and Catherine Sadow
Great Dictations, Interactive Dictations, and **DictationRiddles** by Judy deFilippo and Catherine Sadow

http://www.ProLinguaAssociates.com

EFL/ESL textbooks by Global Stories Press:

Content-based English: Inspiring Solutions (Global Issues series)
Content-based English: Global Stories (Global Issues series)
Content-based English: Humanities (Academic English series)
Content-based English: Science (Academic English series)
Content-based English: Around the World beginner book (Culture series)
Content-based English: Around the World book one (Culture series)
Content-based English: Around the World book two (Culture series)
Responding to Readings One: Life Experiences (beginner)
Responding to Readings Two: Issues (intermediate)

Authentic Readers from the Asians at Work series:

Japanese at Work
Taiwanese at Work
Koreans at Work
Southeast Asians at Work
Chinese at Work

For worksheets and classroom ideas, see the link below:
Asians at Work URL: http://globalstoriespress.com/asians-at-work.html

http://www.GlobalStoriesPress.com